SO-AUF-341

NEW DIRECTIONS FOR EVALUATION
A Publication of the American Evaluation Association

Lois-ellin G. Datta, *Datta Analysis*
EDITOR-IN-CHIEF

WITHDRAWN

Evaluating Country Development Policies and Programs: New Approaches for a New Agenda

Robert Picciotto
The World Bank, Washington, D.C.

Ray C. Rist
George Washington University, Washington, D.C.

EDITORS

THE UNIVERSITY OF TEXAS AT TYLER LIBRARY

Number 67, Fall 1995

JOSSEY-BASS PUBLISHERS
San Francisco

ROBERT R. MUNTZ LIBRARY
THE UNIVERSITY OF TEXAS AT TYLER
TYLER, TEXAS 75701

EVALUATING COUNTRY DEVELOPMENT POLICIES AND PROGRAMS: NEW
APPROACHES FOR A NEW AGENDA
Robert Picciotto, Ray C. Rist (eds.)
New Directions for Evaluation, no. 67
Lois-ellin G. Datta, Editor-in-Chief

© 1995 by Jossey-Bass Inc., Publishers. All rights reserved.

No part of this issue may be reproduced in any form—except for a brief
quotation (not to exceed 500 words) in a review or professional work—
without permission in writing from the publishers.

Microfilm copies of issues and articles are available in 16mm and 35mm,
as well as microfiche in 105mm, through University Microfilms Inc., 300
North Zeeb Road, Ann Arbor, Michigan 48106-1346.

LC 85-644749   ISSN 0164-7989   ISBN 0-7879-9947-4

NEW DIRECTIONS FOR EVALUATION is part of The Jossey-Bass Education
Series and is published quarterly by Jossey-Bass Inc., Publishers, 350
Sansome Street, San Francisco, California 94104-1342.

Subscriptions for 1995 cost $56.00 for individuals and $78.00 for institutions, agencies, and libraries.

EDITORIAL CORRESPONDENCE should be addressed to the Editor-in-Chief,
Lois-ellin G. Datta, P.O. Box 383768, Waikoloa, HI 96738.

Manufactured in the United States of America. Nearly all Jossey-Bass
books, jackets, and periodicals are printed on recycled paper that contains
at least 50 percent recycled waste, including 10 percent postconsumer
waste. Many of our materials are also printed with vegetable-based inks;
during the printing process, these inks emit fewer volatile organic com-
pounds (VOCs) than petroleum-based inks. VOCs contribute to the for-
mation of smog.

New Directions for Evaluation
Sponsored by the American Evaluation Association

EDITOR-IN-CHIEF

Lois-ellin G. Datta   Datta Analysis

ASSOCIATE EDITORS

Jennifer Greene   Cornell University
Gary T. Henry   Georgia State University

EDITORIAL ADVISORY BOARD

Benjamin Alvarez   William Paterson College of New Jersey
Richard A. Berk   University of California, Los Angeles
Donald Bezruki   Legislative Audit Bureau, Wisconsin
Robert F. Boruch   University of Pennsylvania
Roger Brooks   Legislative Audit Bureau, Minnesota
Jonathan Bruel   U.S. Office of Management and Budget
Eleanor Chelimsky   U.S. General Accounting Office
Huey-tsyh Chen   University of Akron
James Earl Davis   University of Delaware
David M. Fetterman   Stanford University
Alan Ginsburg   U.S. Department of Education
James Joseph Heckman   University of Chicago
Larry V. Hedges   University of Chicago
John G. Heilman   Auburn University
Michael Hendricks   MH Associates
Steve Heynneman   The World Bank
Karen C. Holden   University of Wisconsin, Madison
Ernest R. House   University of Colorado
Dionne J. Jones   Pacific Institute for Research and Evaluation
Morris Lai   University of Hawaii, Manoa
Henry M. Levin   Stanford University
Laura C. Leviton   University of Alabama
Richard J. Light   Harvard University
Mark W. Lipsey   Vanderbilt University
Arnold Love   York University
Anna-Marie Madison   University of North Texas
Melvin M. Mark   The Pennsylvania State University
Georg E. Matt   San Diego State University
Ricardo A. Millett   W. K. Kellogg Foundation
Michael Morris   University of New Haven
Stanley Nyirenda   Western Michigan University
Robert Orwin   R.O.W., Inc.
Michael Quinn Patton   Union Institute Graduate School
Emil J. Posavac   Loyola University of Chicago
Sharon Rallis   Regional Laboratory for Educational Improvement,
                             Northeast and Islands
Sharon Ramirez   Rainbow Research, Inc.
Steve W. Raudenbush   Michigan State University
David Rindskopf   City University of New York, Graduate Center
Peter H. Rossi   University of Massachusetts
Robert St. Pierre   Abt Associates
Mary Ann Scheirer   Program Evaluation Consultant, Annandale, Virginia
Michael Scriven   The Evaluation Center, Western Michigan University
Sushil K. Sharma   U.S. General Accounting Office
Richard C. Sonnichsen   Management Consultant, Sand Point, Idaho
Charles L. Thomas   George Mason University
Edith P. Thomas   U.S. Department of Agriculture
Carol H. Weiss   Harvard University
Joseph S. Wholey   U.S. Office of Management and Budget
Robert Yin   COSMOS Corporation

AMERICAN EVALUATION ASSOCIATION, C/O RITA O'SULLIVAN, SCHOOL OF EDUCATION,
UNIVERSITY OF NORTH CAROLINA AT GREENSBORO, GREENSBORO, NORTH CAROLINA 27412

Editorial Policy and Procedures

NEW DIRECTIONS FOR EVALUATION (NDE), a quarterly sourcebook, is an official publication of the American Evaluation Association. NDE publishes empirical, methodological, and theoretical works on all aspects of evaluation and related fields. Substantive areas may include any program, field, or issue with which evaluation is concerned, such as government performance, tax policy, energy, environment, mental health, education, job training, medicine, and public health. Also included are such topics as product evaluation, personnel evaluation, policy analysis, and technology assessment. In all cases, the focus on evaluation is more important than the substantive topics. We are particularly interested in encouraging a diversity of evaluation perspectives and experiences and in expanding the boundaries of our field beyond the evaluation of social programs.

NDE does not consider or publish unsolicited single manuscripts. Each issue of NDE is devoted to a single topic, with contributions solicited, organized, reviewed, and edited by a guest editor. Issues may take any of several forms, such as a series of related chapters, a debate, or a long article followed by brief critical commentaries. In all cases, the proposals must follow a specific format, which can be obtained from the editor-in-chief. These proposals are sent to members of the editorial board and to relevant substantive experts for peer review. The process may result in acceptance, a recommendation to revise and resubmit, or rejection. However, NDE is committed to working constructively with potential guest editors to help them develop acceptable proposals.

Lois-ellin G. Datta, Editor-in-Chief
P.O. Box 383768
Waikoloa, HI 96738

Jennifer C. Greene, Associate Editor
Department of Human Service Studies
Cornell University
Ithaca, NY 14853-4401

Gary Henry, Associate Editor
Public Administration and Urban Studies
Georgia State University
Atlanta, GA 30302-4039

CONTENTS

FROM THE SERIES EDITORS

This year marks two anniversaries: one the "beginning" of systematic evaluations for large-scale programs and the other the establishment of the American Evaluation Association. This first issue of the journal under its new editors includes two changes in masthead in celebration of these events.

Focused Then, A Broader Field Now. In 1965, the first major awards for systematic evaluations of large-scale public investments launched our field. By this reckoning, 1995 is our thirtieth anniversary as a self-conscious discipline. How we have grown over the past three decades! Evaluation began with a focus on programs such as Head Start and the Elementary and Secondary Education Act. Today our members' interests and work have broadened to include evaluations of products, policies, personnel, and practices as well as program evaluation. The first masthead change then is dropping the limiting descriptor "program" from the journal title. The new title, *New Directions for Evaluation,* reflects better the current scope of the field.

One Organization. We celebrate in 1995 our tenth anniversary as the American Evaluation Association (AEA). The Evaluation Network and the Evaluation Research Society merged in 1985. The "General Principles" for the merger included a special agreement covering the first two transition years. In 1986 and 1987, all correspondence and published materials would carry the subname "A Joint Organization of the Evaluation Network and the Evaluation Research Society." In celebrating our first decade as the AEA, it seems appropriate to drop that line from our publications. This change may be a final gesture of putting old divisions behind us. We now recognize on our editorial board page that, however many transitions may be ahead, this transition is successfully behind us. We are one.

Editors' Notes

The deliberations of the 1995 International Evaluation Conference co-sponsored by the American Evaluation Association and the Canadian Evaluation Society will focus on global evaluation issues. Accordingly, this issue of *New Directions for Evaluation* deals with the special evaluation problems of programs being carried out in the zones of turmoil and development where four-fifths of the world's people live.

Economic and social development priorities have been transformed in the last decade. The new development agenda is complex and multifaceted. It poses daunting dilemmas to evaluators working in developing countries and in development agencies. Performance tests previously used have been found wanting, and there is lively debate about new indicators. As policy makers shift their attention away from projects toward programs and policies, evaluation "units of account" have multiplied. Given the conflicting pressures of a more diverse and assertive clientele, evaluation methods are in flux.

Paradoxically, the demands now placed on the evaluation profession are the unintended fruits of its own labors. Sobering results of evaluation studies have bred dissatisfaction with development outcomes. Lessons learned through evaluation have helped to shape the new development agenda, with its emphasis on participation, sustainability, and institutional reform.

Initiatives for reorienting public services—and for reinventing government—have spread throughout the industrialized and the developing world. Given public pressure for improving the sustainability of development programs and projects, development assistance agencies are giving more priority to evaluation.

How then does the new development agenda differ from the policy orientations that underlie traditional evaluation methods? What kinds of adjustments are needed in the approaches, instruments, and processes used by development evaluators? Are the demands for participatory evaluation consistent with the demands for more rigorous evaluation methods and research methods?

The chapters in this volume were discussed in draft form by participants in a Conference on Evaluation and Development hosted by the World Bank in Washington, D.C., in December 1994. The conference brought together development policy makers, practitioners, and evaluators. The resulting collection offers a consistent framework for further debate and proposes new emphases for development evaluation.

Robert Picciotto
Ray C. Rist
Editors

New Directions for Evaluation, no. 67, Fall 1995 © Jossey-Bass Publishers

ROBERT PICCIOTTO is director general of operations evaluation, the World Bank, Washington, D.C.

RAY C. RIST is director of the Center for Policy Studies, Graduate School of Education and Human Development, the George Washington University.

The president of the American Evaluation Association takes stock of progress in the application of evaluation findings to decision making and in the development of evaluation methods. She emphasizes the importance of credibility—through eclecticism in method and clarity of presentation—and of realism, sensitivity, and independence in relationships with decision makers.

Preamble: New Dimensions in Evaluation

Eleanor Chelimsky

Awareness is broadening of the potential of evaluation for improving decision making. A renascent evaluation profession is moving toward expanded use in new topical areas, with wider experience, stronger practice, and greater support by policy makers behind it.

Evaluators in many parts of the world have been honing their methods and seeing their findings used for policy making in ways that would have been inconceivable twenty years ago. Older methods such as survey research, experimental design, or cost-effectiveness analysis are being revamped and adapted to fit different institutions and user needs in countries such as France, Sweden, Colombia, and Tunisia. More recently developed methods such as research synthesis (also known as meta-analysis) are starting to be used widely in Britain, Canada, the Netherlands, and development assistance agencies. Evaluation associations have been formed in Australia, Central and South America, and Europe. The World Bank and other international organizations are establishing a major role in promoting stronger links between planning, program or project effectiveness, and funding. In the United States, Inspector Generals' offices are increasingly developing evaluation branches. Indeed, auditors in developed and developing countries across the world are beginning to include evaluation—which they call "performance audit," or "value-for money audit" or "comprehensive audit"—as one of their key work areas. Furthermore,

An earlier version of this paper was presented to the European Evaluation Society in 1994.

auditors are recognizing more and more that an evaluation is not at all the same thing as an audit.

Today, evaluators feel ready to move on to broader topics of more global interest than those they previously studied. We can now point to a growing number of methodologically successful evaluations that have been well used in policy making, and we are better able to foresee and hurdle at least some of the barriers that have hindered us from influencing policy in the past. We have become more realistic about what evaluation can do in a given policy environment. And we have come to understand better the importance not only of being credible in conducting our evaluations, but of being perceived as credible.

Hence, this paper looks at:

- What we can reasonably expect from evaluation.
- What changes characterize our use of methods today.
- What we have learned about evaluation credibility, and its importance for the use of evaluation findings.

What Evaluation Can and Cannot Do

Logically, evaluation should be useful for most important policy decisions, especially through:

- Synthesizing what is known about a problem and its proposed policy or program remedies.
- Demystifying conventional wisdom or popular myths related either to the problem or its remedies (Max Weber's *entsauberung*).
- Developing new information about program or policy effectiveness.
- Explaining to policy actors the implications of the new information derived through evaluation.

Given a strong evaluation function, it should then be a routine matter to feed objective information to policy makers that can be helpful for their decisions. In practice, however, the decision-making environment and the evaluative process are often so far apart that nothing can bring them together. A government or a development agency may be so profoundly invested in a particular policy that an independent evaluation has few chances of being used or even heard. In the United States during the Vietnam war, for example, the results of evaluations that had been specifically commissioned by the Department of Defense were completely ignored in the very policy process they had been meant to shape. Where evaluation results must compete with really powerful political or institutional goals—such as maintaining control, projecting an image, or saving face—and in almost any specific area where political debates are very hot—abortion or crime in the United States, family planning in China, the condition of women in the Middle East—today's evaluators confront hostilities little different from those that confronted Alexis de Tocqueville in 1847, when he insisted on telling the French Chamber of Deputies what they least wanted to know: that a revolution was on its way.

Another reason evaluation often cannot be helpful is that for many societal problems the basic research has not been done to indicate the best treatment, or at least to present criteria for choosing one treatment over another. Evaluating the impact of a policy, say for reducing urban congestion, is of little use when the hypothetical link between the intervention and its presumed effect has not even been plausibly established by theory and therefore we do not know whether program expectations are reasonable. To what degree should we expect mental health services to reduce depression or despair among AIDS patients? How likely is job training to lead to employment? We may not know the answers to these questions because the basic research has not yet been done into the antecedents of depression among the terminally ill or into the recruitment decisions of employers. Of course, societies are implementing programs, some of them very costly, for mental health or for job training. In such cases, rather than carrying out costly evaluation studies of limited value, evaluators should encourage countries to get the basic research done before setting up comprehensive policies and implementing them widely.

With these difficulties in mind, then, when is it feasible and useful to conduct evaluations and for which types of policy decisions? Evaluation can notably increase the chances of success for three types of decisions:

Formulation and development of a new policy or program. Evaluations of past initiatives can help a policy maker avoid reinventing wheels. They can spare policy makers later political embarrassment by showing early on that the evidence is lacking to warrant the implementation of some highly touted proposal, and they allow policy makers instead to build on earlier interventions that have been effective or promising. The evaluator's role here is to bring to the decision maker the best available information on past experience with the problem to be addressed and on strategies for addressing it.

Assessment, through timely monitoring, of how established programs are doing and of whether the assumptions underlining the policies or programs appear to be correct, or at least not wrong.

Establishment of the results of initiatives, both short-term and long-term, not only to decide whether or how the initiatives should be modified but also to be in a position to defend their proponents' records when election day comes around again.

Evaluators can support these types of decisions today across a very wide spectrum of policy activities—not merely in social policy or program areas as in the past but also in defense, transportation, agriculture, the environment, and almost any other focus of policy.

For evaluation to have a reasonable chance of influencing policy decisions, the necessary basic research must have been done, and political climates and mindsets must be such as to allow policy makers both to hear the results and to use them. Evaluation findings that meet with intense political opposition will have difficulty reaching an audience, at least at first. The recommendations of an unread evaluation stand little chance of being used in decision making.

A more dangerous and debilitating problem for evaluation, however, is that when there is little openness in the user environment and little possibility for dialogue, it is difficult for evaluators to be entirely candid about what they have learned, and there is little incentive for them to try. Yet telling the truth about what has been learned is arguably the most important purpose of evaluation. This is the case not only because of ethics, but because the courage to say what users may not want to hear is the characteristic of an evaluation function that keeps institutions honest. Evaluation does that after the fact, of course, with its findings, but it also does it by dint of its mere presence: just knowing that an independent evaluation is coming—or can be invoked at any time—makes policy makers more prudent and modest in their claims for new programs, more careful in their accountability, more cost conscious, and more willing to do that rare thing in politics: retrace their steps. When evaluators lose their independence, evaluation itself loses much of its purpose, its deterrent value, its credibility, and its power.

This is not an argument against research on politically volatile or controversial topics. First, some research is important to do for its own sake, whether or not its results are used immediately. Second, political situations change, and findings that are unpalatable to one set of decision makers may be ambrosia to their successors. But if we want to pick evaluations—insofar as they can be picked—in such a way as to ensure their success, then we should focus on issues that are of real importance and try to avoid those that are so emotionally charged as to preclude serious debate about the study results.

My own experience is that even when we can abide by this advice, astonishing pressures may build to counter even the most routine, conventional, and unexceptionable evaluations, especially when the evaluation function is just starting out. These pressures may come in the form of efforts to eliminate an evaluation entirely, to change the question being asked to a more "innocuous" one, to soften a report's already very bland language, or to delete individual conclusions and recommendations. Withstanding political pressures obviously requires courage on the part of the evaluator and enough expertise to confront and survive what has become the most typical weapon against "displeasing" findings: the attack on the evaluator's methods. Happily, we know better how to do this today than we did twenty years ago.

Changes in the Use of Evaluation Methods

We look at evaluation methods in the 1990s somewhat differently than we used to, perhaps because so much practical experience in evaluation can now be added to earlier, theoretical perspectives. Though this encounter between theory and practice is transforming both of them in ways that are not yet entirely clear, I believe we are much better off in a number of areas merely because practice has changed.

Complementary Methods. We have learned that every social science method has important weaknesses, but also that the existence of such weaknesses is not fatal. What they imply is a need to use several methods together, so that the strengths of one can compensate for the limitations of the other. We think less today about the absolute merits of one method versus another and more about whether and how using them in concert could result in more conclusive findings.

Emphasis on the Policy Question. We have increased our focus on the question needing to be answered. We have learned that the choice of methods (and of measures and instruments and data) depends much more on the type of question being asked than on the qualities of any particular method. Does the question involve description? Or does it involve reasoning from cause to effect? In a descriptive study, we would not need to worry about the problems of, say, experimental methods because they probably would not be appropriate. In a cause-and-effect study, many different methods might be applicable depending on the policy question.

This centrality of the question, rather than the method, pushes us in the same direction we had to take because of the weaknesses of individual methods: toward method complementarity and reinforcement. For example, we mitigate the superficiality of a survey by adding case studies, we humanize a time-series analysis by conducting a survey or a set of interviews, and we integrate a process evaluation within an outcome study to help explain the results. In the same way, we think of qualitative and quantitative methods together, in terms of how they can strengthen each other, rather than promoting one over the other.

Focusing on the question rather than on the method has liberated us somewhat with regard to our methodological choices and brought a new emphasis on pluralism that sits rather uneasily with the evaluation chapels of our recent past. These chapels were erected to the glory of particular though always fallible methods, each with its own passionate advocates and followers. We can see today that their building has thickened or even created walls between evaluators and the broad range of methodological tools that have always been available to them.

Users' Information Needs. Because policy makers are typically more concerned with the future than the past, evaluators are increasingly committing themselves to prospective studies. Borrowing copiously—or stealing egregiously—from methods used by operations researchers, mathematicians, modelers, and others has gradually enlarged the potential scope of our work, increased its policy relevance, and changed the timing of our interventions. In sum, we now evaluate both ex ante and ex post, and even our retrospective studies now tend to look *also* at future applications of past experience.

Prospective evaluation, especially when used for policy development, can greatly improve the feasibility and performance of new programs. A method that more and more evaluators are adopting for this kind of work is called research synthesis or meta-analysis. This allows the user to get an understanding, relatively quickly, of what has been learned about a particular problem or policy, what has not been learned and needs to be researched, and in which areas there is legitimate disagreement.

Users' Milieu. A greatly increased interest in the users' milieu stems from concern about the use of evaluation findings in policy making. To help ensure that evaluation findings will have an impact, we need to understand what, in the users' organizational or political culture, may promote or prevent their use. Recognizing this, the effort has been to understand where, when, how, and if evaluators can intervene appropriately to facilitate the use of their findings.

The reason we have begun to pay so much attention to our users' milieu is that we have become aware that policy makers and evaluators are quite different with respect to their goals, their standards of evidence, and their tolerance of uncertainty. The evaluator's first goal—knowledge—may be far down on the users' list of priorities. To the user, evidence may merely be instrumental to a negotiation or a decision, whereas to the evaluator, evidence is the end in itself. Evaluators do not invoke certainty unless their data provide such certainty, but policy makers may place positive value on "making a decision," regardless of whether strong objective evidence supports that decision.

Our demystifying job can become extremely difficult. We have to persuade true believers that something they absolutely "know" to be true is in fact hyperbole, myth, unsupported by evidence, or even an outright lie. Spinoza wrote that it is the fact of error that needs explaining, not the discovery of truth. In policy making, however, the truth often is that an error has been made and that policy makers have become invested in that error. Therefore, for evaluators trying to re-establish facts, it is, alas, the truth that needs not only explanation but also very persuasive arguments and data support.

The lesson learned here is that, for evaluation findings to be used in policy making, it is almost as important for evaluators to understand their users—and thereby be able to explain the findings in terms that make sense to them—as it is for the findings to be methodologically strong and compelling in their own right.

Other Changes. First, there has been an increasing recourse to expert panels for setting criteria but no formal consensus on what the criteria should be. Second, we more often find evaluators using frameworks to chart and explain relationships among complex sets of assumptions underlying a problem or a policy. Third, as we have moved to pay more attention to our users' broader information needs, we have seen that "what" and "how" may be as important questions in a policy arena as "why," and that to answer *those* questions, many formerly overlooked population groups are first-rate sources of descriptive information. So we now query practitioners (such as police and teachers) as well as program managers; we seek out patients as well as doctors, farmers as well as economists, crime victims as well as offenders, and program beneficiaries as well as program planners and implementers.

What has happened is that our focus has shifted in search of a more complete picture of reality, a more conclusive answer to a policy question, with the prime objective of improving our ability to inform decision makers. On the other hand, we have to admit that although informing decision makers better is a good thing, getting them to listen is something else entirely. Here we come to the realm of evaluation credibility, which is the capacity of evaluators to make clear, in the user's terms, the objectivity and competence of their work.

Importance of Credibility for the Use of Evaluation Findings

Two types of credibility need to be reflected in an evaluation report. Credibility of substance refers to what has been learned in an evaluation and how it has been learned—whether, for example, distortions have been introduced by the methods chosen and implemented and how those distortions have been accounted for. Substantive credibility establishes the evaluation's objectivity, freedom from bias, nonadvocacy. Credibility of presentation refers to the reporting, rather than the substance, of what has been done: readability, reasonable length, precision of logic and style, and a preference for simple language whenever possible.

Substantive Credibility. If the purpose of conducting an evaluation is to develop new knowledge in the service of policy, then substantive credibility turns principally on the question of what knowledge was produced and how it was acquired. Credibility here concerns how an evaluation establishes what is known, what is uncertain, and what is not known, as well as the strength of the evidence relating to all three.

Evaluators use a number of methods to enhance credibility, but three of them are, I think, critical because together they demonstrate the effort that has been made in an evaluation to establish the quality of the knowledge gained. The first of these methods, the literature review, serves four credibility purposes: it helps establish the expertise of the evaluators; it situates the evaluation with respect to past work in the area; it sets the stage for showing precisely what new information has been developed by the evaluation; it helps to demonstrate objectivity in the way the evaluators deal with work featuring viewpoints and methodologies different from their own. Put another way, one-sided presentations of past evaluative work always arouse suspicions of bias among readers who know the literature. Indeed, a first check on the quality of an evaluation is the quality of the literature review summarized in the report.

A second way of establishing substantive credibility is through appropriate self-criticism in the methodology discussion. Take, for example, experimental design methods. Although they can confer the precious benefit of conclusiveness, they have weaknesses that are by now very well known, especially their inflexibility and the gaps they leave in our understanding of program or policy effectiveness. Nonetheless, as I mentioned earlier, we continue to use these designs, or a quasi-experimental alternative, complementing their limitations by the strengths of other methods, and we build credibility for these designs through candor about both their benefits and their limitations.

We tell the reader, for example, how we handled the relevant threats to validity and what we could not do that we thought was necessary or desirable. For example, if the user's timeline or a shortage of resources prevented us from carefully ruling out an explanation for the findings that would have been a plausible alternative to the one presented in the report, we say so, and we also note the implications for the policy use of the findings. What we have learned is that a low response rate in survey research, or the lack of generalizability in unstructured qualitative research, constitutes less of a problem for credibility than failing to mention them and to discuss their implications for policy.

A third way we enhance credibility today comes from trying to foresee the potential political and methodological attacks on the evaluation's findings. This allows us to build in—as early as the design stage—both the ability to show the strength of our findings and to respond competently to the attacks. In short, substantive credibility derives from the reader's perception that the evaluators have been expert in their task and honest about their findings and methodology.

Still, competence and candor are only half the battle: we must reflect them in our writing but at the same time avoid what Cronbach calls "self-defeating thoroughness." To an evaluator, all data are important and all technical details are fascinating. But the policy maker, instead of being fascinated, just stops reading, believing like Voltaire that the "secret of being a truly great bore is to tell everything."

Presentational Credibility. No matter how objective and expert the actual conduct of an evaluation may have been, this can be entirely misperceived if the work is carelessly presented. Our goal in reporting evaluation findings should be to enable our users to understand, quickly, without long phrases or high-sounding words, all those things that it took us so many pains and such considerable cost to learn over the course of years. In an evaluation report, at a minimum, we need to communicate four things effectively to our readers:

- The precise questions the evaluation sought to answer
- The methods that were used to answer them
- The major strengths and weaknesses in the study's design and execution, and the efforts made to compensate for the weaknesses
- The findings of the study, how conclusive they are, whether or why they are important, how they fit with prior evaluation findings, and where and how they should be applied

Technical appendixes to a report meet the need for precision while allowing the report proper to keep technical talk to a minimum. They leave room for a lengthy discussion of what, for example, the evaluators did to avoid various types of bias in their data, but they do not interfere with the policy-related "story line" spelled out in the report proper. Accompanying a report with an oral briefing for policy makers is an effective way to present what has been learned by the evaluation and to communicate a policy message targeted to the user's information need.

Credibility is worth almost any effort because it wins the evaluator a fair hearing, an interested (even greatly expanded) audience, survival to speak another day, and a much greater likelihood that the work will be used and will matter in policy making.

Conclusion

Though evaluators still have difficulty getting their voices heard when policies are highly controversial, the general pattern of recent evaluation experience is one of surmounting past problems and of improvements both in practice and in decision makers' support for evaluation. We now have the technical capability to address policy questions concerning many different topical areas in a productive way that is useful to our sponsors. We can also take on more complex, ambitious policy questions than in the past.

The question before us is no longer can we do evaluations, but rather, why aren't more of them done? Big changes in institutions usually come slowly. They take a lot of preparation, commitment, and hard work. Just creating a successful evaluation function means bringing together skilled evaluators and helping them understand each other; choosing topics to evaluate that are both important in a policy sense and evaluable; finding the time, funding, and user commitment to do the job properly; protecting the independence of the function; supporting evaluators in fighting against distortion of their findings; and ensuring that evaluators understand the culture and information needs of sometimes far-away users, on whom the impact of their findings may depend.

It is not easy for evaluators and policy makers to learn how to work together. Although we have seen a good deal of successful coordinated practice lately, and although the future of the partnership now seems quite promising, I would still advise any evaluator to remember that when the lion and the calf lie down together, the calf isn't likely to get much sleep.

Perhaps the greatest accomplishment of evaluation today is that credible evaluations are conducted on a regular basis, their findings are typically incorporated into policy, and they are being done more and more as a part of routine organizational practice. As evaluation spreads internationally, and as political support for it develops, it may be that we will at long last get our chance to see evaluation do what it was intended to do: help make institutions more effective, more responsive, more trusted, more accountable, and even—who knows?—better managed.

ELEANOR CHELIMSKY *is president of the American Evaluation Association. She was assistant comptroller-general, United States General Accounting Office.*

Over the past two decades, development priorities have been funda-
mentally reshaped. Evaluation has contributed to this redesign and a
remarkable consensus has emerged among development practitioners.
In turn, the new directions of development policy have created fresh
challenges for evaluation.

Introduction: Evaluation and Development

Robert Picciotto

This introductory chapter explores the intersection between evaluation and development. The two activities are closely intertwined: learning is a major objective of evaluation and, in many respects, development is all about learning too.

A Time for Stock Taking

Now that development and evaluation have logged about fifty years of practice, this is a propitious time for recollection. Especially during the past two decades, development programs and projects have been subject to searching scrutiny by professional evaluators. Hard-won experience from thousands of development schemes has been documented and fed back into the design of development policies. Conversely, given the requirements of emerging development priorities, the methods, products, and processes of evaluation are in urgent need of reexamination.

Evaluation is no stranger to change: it is a young, diverse, and freewheeling profession. Nowhere is this more evident than in development evaluation, where the auditing tradition of evaluation is far less influential than its social science antecedents. It will take time and effort for development evaluators to converge on a common approach to methodology and practice adapted to the new development agenda. Beyond the broad evaluation principles endorsed by the Organization for Economic Cooperation and Development's Development Assistance Committee (1992), international agreement about specific development evaluation guidelines has proven elusive, and the International

Organization of Supreme Audit Institutions (INTOSAI) has only recently started work on program evaluation standards.

A major obstacle to achieving quick consensus lies in the unsettled state of development theory. From the 1950s to the 1970s, development economics provided a ready-made theoretical foundation for the evaluation of development programs and projects. Its subsequent decline (Krugman, 1994) left a void that neither neoclassicism nor the nascent institutional economics has yet been able to fill.

This said, it may well be that no single discipline can be expected to dominate in an endeavor that deals with the multiple challenges, hopes, and exertions of the majority of humankind. In the absence of a single intellectual rallying point, trespassing across disciplinary boundaries is common and evaluators are increasingly eclectic and venturesome in their use of social science instruments.

Thus, this is a time for reflection and debate. Accordingly, this chapter provides a backdrop for a much-needed reconsideration of development evaluation approaches and practices. First, it offers a brief retrospective of development thinking, then outlines the new development agenda, and finally highlights some implications for development evaluation.

The Development Record

It has been fifty years since World War II ended and the victorious industrial democracies announced their determination to turn swords into ploughshares. In the wake of the breakup of colonial empires in Asia and Africa, modernization was viewed as a straightforward, hopeful process, and development assistance was conceived as a global fight against poverty, ignorance, and disease (American Academy of Arts and Sciences, 1989).

These high ideals animated a development crusade that attracted thousands of recruits and commanded vast resources. Systems analysts and social scientists embraced the new development field and assembled a toolkit for the assessment of development programs and projects. Armed with cost/benefit analysis and operational research instruments, evaluation pioneers ascribed virtually no limits to the exercise of rationality in the realm of human affairs.

In parallel, a new branch of economics—focusing on growth and social transformation—emerged and held the academic limelight for about two decades (Meier and Seers, 1984). Scores of bilateral and multilateral agencies were created to act as shunting yards for skills and resources. Thousands of development projects were designed, funded, and implemented. Ideological competition pitting the capitalist countries against the communist bloc helped to fuel this momentum.

A Remarkable Record. Given its vast ambition, the development enterprise proceeded by fits and starts and left some parts of the world behind, but the overall record has been one of extraordinary advance in living standards.

To a remarkable extent, the heady self-confidence of the development pioneers proved self-fulfilling.

In the aggregate, the economic progress of developing countries has been phenomenal. As Sven Sandstrom, World Bank managing director, said in inaugurating the 1994 Conference on Evaluation and Development, "We know that there has been faster progress in improving the human condition over the last fifty years than during the entire previous span of history. A child born in the developing world today . . . can expect to earn an income more than double that of a child born just a generation ago."

Between 1960 and 1990, average life expectancy increased by six months each year, infant mortality dropped by more than half, food production rose much faster than population, malnutrition was reduced by more than 40 percent, and adult literacy grew by 50 percent. From the mid 1960s until 1990, developing countries outperformed high-income countries in terms of gross domestic product growth, averaging 5 percent annual growth compared to 3.7 percent growth in high-income countries. Excluding Europe and Central Asia, the growth since 1990 has been even more impressive—at 4.7 percent annually compared to 1.2 percent in high-income countries (World Bank, 1994a).

Such economic and social advances are especially impressive against the background of the population explosion with which developing countries have had to contend. Over the past two decades, 1.6 billion people have been added to the world's population, more than lived on the planet at the beginning of this century; developing countries contributed about 90 percent of the increment.

A Job Still Unfinished. Given the unprecedented achievements of development in the face of awesome economic and social obstacles, it is paradoxical that the current mood should be one of unease and uncertainty. Why has the glow associated with early development efforts dimmed? In part, the disillusionment arises out of the realization that, even with all the progress achieved, more than a billion people still live in abject poverty, on one dollar a day or less. Seven million people die every year from easily preventable diseases. Child mortality is still ten times higher in developing countries than in developed countries. Maternal death rates are thirty times higher. Nearly half of the people of South Asia and sub-Saharan Africa still live in poverty.

Although more people have been lifted out of poverty over the last generation than in any previous generation, more people live in poverty today than at any time in history. Poverty reduction remains a formidable task. Faced with an apparently Sisyphean challenge, the patience of the industrial country electorates—on whom development assistance funding ultimately depends—is wearing thin, just at a time when an increasingly integrated global economic and physical environment calls for stronger development cooperation.

The Problem of Failing States. What dominates perceptions is not the untold story of developing countries acting as the engine of global growth, but rather the unfinished poverty reduction agenda. Public disappointment may be related to misperceptions about the potential of external assistance to overcome, in short order, deep-seated economic and social obstacles—or even to simple ignorance. A recent poll of the attitudes of U.S. citizens disclosed a median estimate of U.S. spending on foreign aid of 15 percent of the budget, compared to an actual level of less than 1 percent (Kinsley, 1995).

In addition, there is declining public trust in government and a perception that the developing world is in deep crisis. Undoubtedly, with the unfreezing of history caused by the end of the cold war, the basic premise of development—the existence of a functioning state—no longer holds in a growing number of countries plagued by ethnic conflict and civil strife. With rising anarchy, the most basic rights (including the right to life) are abused and there is a domino effect as violence, disease, and refugees spill over international borders. Never mind that government breakdown and social disintegration are the exception rather than the rule. Bad news commands the media's attention, crowding out good news of advances in the world's wellbeing and spreading democracy (with, for example, more than thirty national elections held in sub-Saharan Africa over the past five years). The perception that entire states are failing is new because until recently such events were masked by the East-West conflict. In the old world order, bilateral support propped up failing states irrespective of development outcomes. Today, situations are left unattended until humanitarian and peacekeeping actions become imperative, feeding the misconception that the development enterprise itself is hopeless.

Ironically, these circumstances have led to a diversion of resources from development to the management of humanitarian crises. Yet, it is precisely the lack of timely assistance to deal with economic mismanagement, galloping population growth, lack of employment opportunities, and environmental degradation that often lies at the root of civil strife and social disintegration. Although curative measures are more costly than preventive development actions, they command more commitment from developed countries, which, in the absence of a crisis or a unifying threat affecting their own interests, prefer to direct scarce fiscal resources to resolving domestic problems.

Differentiated Performance. Another sobering factor is the growing thirst for public accountability and the resulting scrutiny of government expenditure programs, in developed and developing countries alike. This has meant a sharper concern for development effectiveness and a reduced role for ideology in the management of development assistance. This public mood helps to explain the greater selectivity being pursued in the provision of development assistance. With shrinking public tolerance for ineffectual use of aid, the development agenda has become more ambitious and demanding. The reshaping of development priorities also reflects evaluation findings that point to the inadequacy of government-led development strategies that are poorly adapted to the integrated global economy.

The New Development Agenda

Policy. Uneven development performance among developing countries became highly visible with the sharply increased volatility of the global economy in the 1970s and the resulting debt crisis. These vicissitudes (and the risks they posed to the financial system) put the spotlight on the collective cost of economic distortions and confirmed the crucial role of sound macroeconomic management in ensuring sustained improvement in living standards. Specifically, the vast differences in economic performance between East Asia (which averaged per capita GDP growth of 4 to 7 percent annually between 1966 and 1993) and Latin America (with per capita GDP growth of 0 to 4 percent over the same period) brought to light the crucial role of stable prices, sound fiscal policy, and open trade in delivering sustained and efficient growth. They also emphasized the critical role of government in contributing to economic and social progress through concentration on what only governments can do—investment in people and the creation of a suitable environment for the private sector (World Bank, 1991).

Whereas most pioneers of development economics had promoted the primacy of economic planning and import substitution policies, the upshot of the debt crisis highlighted the limits of state involvement in the economy and demonstrated the vast superiority of outward-looking, flexible economic policies. This triggered a resurgence of neoclassical economics and, in parallel, a concerted international effort to help developing countries rectify major imbalances in their economies. Hence, development assistance was redirected from investment projects to policy adjustment.

Capacity Building. The debt crisis and the "miracle" of rapid development in East Asian countries contributed to a broad consensus regarding economic fundamentals and a "market friendly" (as well as "people friendly") role for the state. Meanwhile, the crucial importance of public sector reform and capacity building emerged starkly from the evaluation of development assistance programs directed to sub-Saharan Africa, the only region of the world where, despite improved socioeconomic indicators, per capita growth has been negligible or negative for the past two decades. Military conflict, civil strife, weak institutions, slow human resource development, and an undeveloped private sector—combined with an adverse policy environment—have translated into low average returns to investment and a dismal development record for the region (Husain, 1994).

Perhaps the scarcest ingredient of development in this part of the world has been the capacity to design and implement policy, to create a suitable environment for private enterprises, and to manage basic government services. Hence, it is not surprising that the term "governance" was first used in a development context in a long-term perspective study of sub-Saharan Africa (World Bank, 1990).

This said, country performance has differed considerably within the region. Over the past five years, twenty-one countries in sub-Saharan Africa (almost half of the countries in the region) experienced positive per capita growth and, of these, just over half reached or exceeded a 4 to 5 percent growth rate in GDP. At the other end of the spectrum, twenty countries experienced negative growth rates and pulled the average in the region down; several of these countries were plagued by civil war or social unrest.

The threefold lesson from this experience—peace and tranquillity matter, policy matters, institutions matter—has been confirmed in the vastly different context of the former Soviet Union. With the implosion of Soviet power and the emergence of many newly independent countries in Europe and Central Asia, the diversity and complexity of the development enterprise has acquired new dimensions. Although the formerly socialist states have made major investments in their human capital, they too lack the basic institutional infrastructure needed to operate a modern market economy. Accordingly, capacity building now holds center stage in development assistance, a throwback to the basic "nation building" preoccupations of the development pioneers.

The Sustainability Challenge. The integration of the "second world" within the international economic system facilitated the global adoption of a coherent set of economic management principles worldwide: the new development agenda. The prominence of environmental considerations within this agenda is linked, in no small part, to the disclosure that central planning has caused much damage to the natural environment of Eastern Europe and the former Soviet Union, given its relentless focus on physical measures of output, unresponsiveness to local concerns, and overreliance on lagging technologies.

Environmental distresses in the southern hemisphere (symbolized by the shrinking rainforest) and in eastern Europe (of which Chernobyl is emblematic) are distinct, but their severity and sudden visibility have helped to create a new awareness of the looming problems that threaten the global commons. This challenge has been articulated with vigor and skill by nongovernmental organizations. Pressures on the environment have mounted over the past fifty years. At the local level, nearly two billion people lack access to adequate sanitation while 1.3 billion suffer from indoor pollution, and water resources are under growing stress. On a planetary scale, there has been more change since 1950 than between 8000 B.C. and 1950. Loss of tree cover (200 million hectares since 1970, an area the size of the United States east of the Mississippi); extinction of thousands of plant and animal species; loss of nearly 500 billion tons of topsoil (equivalent to India's cropland); and air pollution reaching health-threatening levels in hundreds of cities are among the indicators that, according to Herman Daly, a former World Bank staff member, suggest that the earth is being treated as if it were a business in liquidation.

Under pressure from public opinion, major shifts in the development business are underway to reflect increased sensitivity to the environment. The working definition of sustainable development offered by Norwegian Prime Minister Gro Harlem Brundtland has been widely endorsed: "Development that meets the needs of the present without compromising the ability of future generations to meet their own needs" (World Commission on Environment and Development, 1987). Considerable debate remains between environmental activists and development practitioners about the specific policy implications of the environmental challenge. Many nongovernmental organizations would slow down or even interrupt economic growth in order to alleviate environmental damage. Most development professionals, on the other hand, see considerable scope for "win-win" policies combining growth and sustainability (World Bank, 1992a). The debate is still young, however, and reliable evidence from evaluation is still scarce.

The New Agenda. After five decades of concerted attention to the challenge of development, the underlying concepts have changed. Gone are the days when development was conceived mostly in terms of centrally planned investments, when governments were expected to exercise strict control over the commanding heights of the economy, when development programming was managed with input-output models, or when development assistance was geared to the financing of discrete investment projects. Today, development is viewed as a participatory process; governments are expected to concentrate on developing human resources and creating market-friendly regulatory environments; development assistance increasingly focuses on policy and capacity building, while preoccupation with public expenditures focuses more on restraint than on expansion. This reorientation of development priorities toward sustainability and institutional development is based in no small part on the findings of evaluation (World Bank, Operations Evaluation Department).

To sum up, the overarching priority of the new development agenda is sustainable poverty reduction through a three-pronged strategy: (1) a policy framework geared to broadly based and stable economic growth; (2) investment in people; and (3) institutional reform to promote private sector development and participation.

A sound policy framework is essential. In this connection, five major lessons have been learned through policy research and evaluation. First, only market-based growth strategies improve living standards on a sustainable basis. Second, growth that is not anchored to sound economic management fundamentals is shortlived and hurts the poor disproportionately. Third, growth policies that do not make use of the poor's main asset—labor—are ineffective in reducing poverty. Fourth, public expenditure policies that do not give priority to productive infrastructure, targeted social programs, and safety nets to vulnerable groups are not socially sustainable. Fifth, win-win links between growth, poverty reduction, and environmental protection must be forged through well-conceived policies and public expenditure programs.

Investment in people is just as important as good policies. For the poor to contribute to (and benefit from) growth, basic education, health, and nutrition services are essential. Together with family planning, these help reduce the rate of population growth and raise the productivity of the economy. Broadly based poverty reduction also requires that special attention be directed to the participation of women in development. In most developing countries, women play major roles as producers of food, protectors of the environment, and educators of the young. They make up a quarter of the work force. Yet they have all too often been invisible in development programs.

Last but not least, the reorientation of institutions and the concurrent construction of domestic capacities are essential to sustainable and equitable development. A new role for the state is needed to unleash the energies of the private sector and of the civil society, through decentralization, deregulation, and debureaucratization. Improved economic governance through accountability, transparency, and the rule of law has become a central objective of development assistance (World Bank, 1994b).

Implications for Evaluation

According to Tom Peters, "what gets measured, gets done." Therefore, when a line of business faces fundamental changes, the standards against which it evaluates its performance must change as well. As long as public expenditure was perceived as the major engine of development, the discrete investment project provided a convenient channel for development assistance, and cost/benefit analysis dominated development evaluation. Solidly grounded in welfare economics, cost/benefit analysis bridges macroeconomic modelling and investment programming; shadow pricing takes account of distortions in the policy environment while sensitivity analysis helps to assess the potential impact of price changes and other risks.

Once the investment-led development model lost its dominance and the new growth economics, emphasizing the role of policy, knowledge, and institutions, became influential, cost/benefit analysis lost its privileged status in development evaluation. As a result, analytical talent drifted away to deal with the design of adjustment programs, the surveillance of macroeconomic policy, and the management of multidisciplinary teams focused on capacity-building assignments geared to thematic concerns (poverty reduction, private sector development, and environmental protection).

There is broad consensus about the "what" of the new development agenda but much debate about the "how" (relative emphasis among multiple objectives, sequencing, institutional implications, and so on). Considerable innovation is underway. Multiple development objectives, multifaceted operations, and a diversified set of instruments (ranging from discrete investment projects through sector programs and thematic capacity development interventions to policy adjustment operations) characterize today's development assistance business. In this postmodern environment, the spare architecture of Little-Mirrlees and Squire–Van der Tak no longer towers over the intellectual skyline. Development evaluators are drawing from all the social science disciplines and tapping into the rich lode of evaluation experience from developed countries.

This is the broad context in which development practitioners are engaged in a far-reaching reexamination of the relevance and effectiveness of their business practices and processes. Since the World Bank (1992b) issued its report on the need to reform its portfolio management and evaluation system, most multilateral and bilateral development agencies have initiated similar reassessments.

Reevaluating Evaluation. What then are the main directions of reform in the development evaluation field? Three major areas of concern cut across the chapters collected in this issue. They concern frameworks, skills, and structure. Evaluation frameworks focus increasingly on development impact. Most development practitioners and stakeholders view results on the ground and sustainability as the acid tests of performance. Accordingly, evaluators are giving greater attention to *impact* assessments carried out several years after investment completion. This decreases reliance on notoriously unreliable projections of benefits and allows direct verification of the resilience of institutional arrangements. On the other hand, it extends the feedback loop for lesson learning and greatly complicates the evaluation task. Specifically, as highlighted by George Psacharopoulos in Chapter Six, this option involves a tradeoff of relevance for accuracy. Consequently, it is not uncommon for new evaluation work programs to combine more work on impact evaluations with greater stress on feedback and dissemination activities and/or more process evaluations specifically designed to improve quality management and guide business process innovations.

The focus on evaluation feedback reflects a growing impatience with the documented weaknesses of ex ante evaluation processes that govern the quality of new projects. In Chapter Four, James Winpenny argues that appraisal optimism, environmental astigmatism, inadequate valuation of side effects, and other biases could lead to a "survival of the least environmentally fit" among development projects unless the focus of project evaluation shifts radically toward serving a more responsive project cycle. He notes that similar problems affect the processing of projects in all sectors.

There is considerable ferment with respect to the instruments of evaluation. At a time of increased concern with the effectiveness of development programs and projects, measurement of development results on the basis of a set of predetermined and quantifiable performance indicators exerts a powerful appeal, even though, ironically, standard cost/benefit analysis is falling into disuse. Krishna Kumar warns in Chapter Five about the limits of complex indicator systems where development programs are experimental and process-based or where data requirements are wont to over stress developing country administrative resources.

On the other hand, William Branson and Carl Jayarajah show, in Chapter Two, that it is feasible to assess complex macroeconomic adjustment programs by assessing the impact of each policy instrument in terms of the behavior of the target variable that is most sensitive to that instrument. Similarly, at the sector level, Stephen Mayo argues compellingly in Chapter Eight that well-selected indicators geared to sector-level performance can provide a unique diagnostic capacity regarding the need for policy reform, the identification of best practice, and the monitoring of development interventions.

Thus, given the shifts in perspectives imposed by "units of account," which transcend individual projects, quantitative methods are growing ever more sophisticated. Conversely, given the advent of participatory development, the instruments of evaluation are in a state of flux. At the micro level, the preoccupation with a single measure of net present worth has given way to qualitative approaches, including such practical guides toward interaction with beneficiaries as the logical framework, participatory rural appraisals, and beneficiary assessments. In Chapter Ten, Lawrence Salmen provides convincing evidence of the power of listening. In Chapter Eleven, Samuel Paul shows how client surveys can have an energizing effect on the management of public service monopolies.

At the same time, proponents of the scientific approach such as Lyn Squire, in Chapter One, argue that only experimental (or in certain circumstances quasi-experimental) techniques can deal with the counterfactual problem in a convincing way. Bridging these approaches, Caroline Moser in Chapter Seven proposes a combination of evaluation techniques (for example, intrahousehold surveys, community surveys) to throw light on social transformation processes, as a complement to quantitative impact indicators.

Given the above trends, the *skills* involved in evaluation are becoming more specialized and diverse. Using the classification of the Greek poet Archilocus, it would seem that modern evaluation needs hedgehogs (they know a lot about one thing) as well as foxes (they know a little about many things). For example, analysis of the legal framework is a fundamental ingredient of organizational evaluation according to Thomas Stanton, who shows in Chapter Three that the choice of instrumentality for achieving a development purpose requires a keen understanding of the performance potential and limitations imposed by the legal environment. Taking culture into account is even trickier. Robert Klitgaard's contribution, Chapter Nine, makes clear how cultural factors condition the success of alternative institutional options. However, discovering the right variables and interpreting them is demanding, and recent intellectual advances have only begun to produce operationally relevant findings; anthropologists are, apparently, not yet as useful as soil scientists, and there remains a need for evaluation generalists to help synthesize contrasting disciplinary perspectives.

Evaluation *structure* continues to pose difficult choices. Notwithstanding the good intentions of the development agenda about development effectiveness and sustainability, there is no guarantee that the managers and staff of development organizations (or developing country agencies) will take systematic account of evaluation findings, however relevant. Neither does managerial awareness of the importance of evaluation translate automatically into the requisite organizational setup. For evaluation to fulfill its unique potential, a subtle combination of independence and constructive engagement is needed to contribute to professional excellence through continuous organizational learning. In other words, Say's Law does not apply fully: good evaluation does not always create its own demand. Demand must be nurtured in parallel.

Of course, evaluation demand extends beyond the boundaries of any single organization. A good evaluation study can have positive spillover effects throughout the development community. Development evaluation has the characteristics of an international public good. Given the misconceptions that prevail about development, objective development evaluations deserve widespread dissemination. Finally, given the power of ideas to promote growth and policy reform, poor countries should not be denied the resources needed to build their own domestic evaluation capacities.

References

American Academy of Arts and Sciences. "A World to Make: Development in Perspective." *Journal of the American Academy of Arts and Sciences*, 1989, *118* (1).

Husain, I. *The Challenge of Africa*. Washington, D.C.: World Bank, 1994.

Kinsley, M. "The Intellectual Free Lunch." *New Yorker*, Feb. 6, 1995.

Krugman, P. "The Fall and Rise of Development Economics." In L. Rodwin and D. A. Schon (eds.), *Rethinking the Development Experience*. Washington, D.C.: Brookings Institution and the Lincoln Institute, 1994.

Little, I.M.D., and Mirrlees, J. A. *Project Appraisal and Planning for Developing Countries*. New York: Basic Books, 1974.

Meier, G. M., and Seers, D. *Pioneers in Development Economics*. Washington, D.C., and London: Oxford University Press for the World Bank, 1984.

Organization for Economic Cooperation and Development (OECD). *Development Assistance Manual: Development Assistance Committee Principles for Effective Aid*. Paris: Organization for Economic Cooperation and Development, 1992.

Squire, L., and Van der Tak, H. *Economic Analysis of Projects*. Baltimore, Md.: Johns Hopkins University Press for the World Bank, 1975.

World Bank. *Sub-Saharan Africa: From Crisis to Sustainable Growth*. Washington, D.C.: World Bank, 1989.

World Bank. *Long-Term Perspective Study of Sub-Saharan Africa*. Washington, D.C.: World Bank, 1990.

World Bank. *The Challenge of Development: World Development Report, 1991*. Washington D.C.: World Bank, 1991.

World Bank. *Development and the Environment: World Development Report, 1992*. Washington, D.C.: 1992a.

World Bank. *Effective Implementation: Key to Development Impact*. Report of the World Bank's Portfolio Management Task Force. Washington, D.C.: World Bank, 1992b.

World Bank. *Global Economic Prospects and the Developing Countries*. Washington, D.C.: World Bank, 1994a.

World Bank. *Governance: The World Bank's Experience*. Washington, D.C.: World Bank, 1994b.

World Bank, Operations Evaluation Department (OED). *Evaluation Results*. Washington, D.C.: World Bank, 1988, 1989, 1990, 1991, 1992, 1993.

World Commission on Environment and Development. *Our Common Future*. New York: Oxford University Press, 1987.

ROBERT PICCIOTTO *is director general of operations evaluation, the World Bank, Washington, D.C.*

PART ONE

Frameworks for Evaluation

*This chapter discusses the necessary ingredients for rigorous evalua-
tion of poverty alleviation programs in developing countries. It con-
fronts such poverty-specific issues as empowerment of the poor,
beneficiary participation in design and implementation of programs,
and beneficiary assessments.*

Evaluating the Effectiveness of Poverty Alleviation Programs

Lyn Squire

For the purpose of this chapter, evaluation is defined as an effort to gather evidence on the costs and benefits of programs with the objective of guiding the
design and implementation of future programs or improving the ones being
evaluated. Also in this context, poverty alleviation programs are understood to
encompass all interventions designed specifically to improve the living standards of the poor. Although this definition is broadly interpreted to include
income-generating projects, social sector programs, and infrastructure projects,
as well as efforts to empower the poor, it excludes programs and policies
designed to encourage broad-based growth even though such growth is critical to any strategy to reduce poverty (World Bank, 1990a). By the same token,
it excludes efforts to evaluate the poverty-reducing impact of overall development strategies even though "poverty assessments" encouraged by the World
Bank and others are becoming increasingly common.

Evaluation as defined in this chapter is used sparingly in developing countries. One reason is that evaluation has often suffered from defects that limit
its usefulness. This is especially true with regard to poverty alleviation programs, where such issues as gender, intrahousehold allocation, the role of
extended families, and unequal power relationships complicate the task of the
evaluator.

The primary purpose of this chapter is to show how the *fundamentals* of
evaluation apply to poverty alleviation programs. To this end, the chapter
explores poverty-specific issues, such as empowerment of the poor and beneficiary participation. It also discusses qualitative approaches to evaluation, such
as participant observation and beneficiary assessment, as well as quantitative,

econometric, and experimental approaches. The chapter is organized around four fundamental questions:

What is the program objective? Improvement in the living standards of the poor is the ultimate goal of all poverty programs, but an adequate indicator of that objective is elusive. As a result, evaluations often operate with an intermediate objective, which in turn emerges from an understanding of *why* people are poor in the specific program context. Clarity on the intermediate objective is important for proper evaluation.

How should program impact be measured? Program impact should be judged against what would have happened in the program's absence. Thus, evaluation requires specification of a counterfactual. Because the counterfactual is not observed, the technique for specifying it requires careful thought.

What constitutes a program for the purposes of evaluation? An evaluation focused exclusively on inputs (budget costs, for example) and outputs (reflecting intermediate objectives such as student performance) might fail to account for the often critical role of other factors—especially within-program incentives and institutional arrangements—and thus lead to inaccurate conclusions. A meaningful evaluation should incorporate all the key factors influencing outcomes.

What programs should evaluators examine? Resources for evaluation are scarce and need to be allocated to activities with the highest return. Due consideration should be given to the likely impact of the evaluation and its cost.

Each of these four questions is addressed below.

Objective

This section explores two issues to illustrate the importance of clear objectives. The first involves a comparison between two programs—one designed to transfer income and the other designed to create assets. The comparison demonstrates a simple but fundamental point: different objectives require different evaluations. The second has to do with the empowerment of the poor, an increasingly important intermediate objective. This raises fundamental questions about the determination of program goals and their evaluation.

Income Transfer and Asset Creation. To illustrate how the intermediate objective of a program stems from an understanding of why the poor are poor and how it leads to different evaluations, consider the case of the Bolivia Emergency Social Fund (ESF) and its successor institution, the Social Investment Fund (SIF). The former is a good example of a program designed to transfer income, and the latter of a program designed to create assets.

Established in December 1986, the ESF was charged with the task of providing emergency relief and carrying out an employment-generating economic reactivation program designed to assist the population groups most acutely affected by the economic crisis. The rationale in this case is clear—the economy had been in decline since 1980 and was experiencing severe unemployment and loss of income following the introduction of the New Economic

Policy in mid 1985 (with its attendant fiscal and monetary austerity) and the collapse of tin prices later in the year. Having identified a particular reason why the poor were suffering, the program was designed to offset some of the short-run costs of economic decline and adjustment through the provision of employment-generating activities.

By 1990 attention was turning from the immediate needs of the economic emergency to the issue of long-run development. SIF was established in January 1990 to mobilize external assistance for the social sectors and to extend coverage of health, education, and water and sanitation services to more of the poor (World Bank, 1990b). The need identified was access to various services rather than access of the poor to employment opportunities. To meet this need SIF established a mechanism to provide physical assets to poor communities. The approach included a strong element of community participation in decision making.

Different objectives call for different approaches to evaluation. In the case of ESF, the issue for evaluation was to determine the extent to which the funded subprojects had generated higher levels of employment earnings and at what cost. In the case of the SIF, the issue for evaluation was to determine the extent to which the funded subprojects had improved the health status and educational attainment of the poor and at what cost. Impact evaluations focused on these different outcomes. Evaluation of ESF used household data on labor income to show that the weekly earnings of the average participant were 50 percent higher than they would have been in the absence of the program (Newman, Jorgensen, and Pradhan, 1991). Evaluation of SIF, on the other hand, used several measures of impact, such as child mortality, nutritional status, school matriculation, and academic achievement (Coa, 1992).

Empowerment. The evaluation procedures described above require prior specification of an objective. An understanding of broad economic developments in Bolivia helped fashion the programs described above, but increasingly poverty alleviation programs are trying to empower the poor so that the poor can help in determining program objectives. This raises some new questions for evaluation.

Consider the Municipal Funds component of the Decentralization and Regional Development Project in Mexico. This project transfers to municipalities funds that can then be invested in a wide range of small projects—for example, water supply, rural roads, and school rehabilitation. Investments are selected in conjunction with the community Solidarity Committee (World Bank, 1994).

As argued above, each program should be assessed relative to its objective. In this case, if the objective is to elicit the preferences of the local community in setting priorities, then it will be useful to evaluate the mechanism—voting, discussion groups—used to ensure that the selected combination of investments truly reflects the interests of all members of the community. Various diagnostic studies can serve this purpose (Valadez and Bamberger, forthcoming). They may include the use of quantitative indicators, such as the number of meetings, attendance at meetings, frequency of votes, as well as qualitative assessments on the extent to which individuals believed that their views had been heard and the process was fair. Evaluation of the Municipal Funds showed that in the majority of cases, poor rural communities actively participated in the selection, but in some instances the selection process had not been especially open or had been overly influenced by local or state officials.

The preceding discussion focuses on the evaluation of the program's intermediate objective—the empowerment of the poor—but the program also results in the creation of assets, which also require evaluation. For this task a distinction may have to be made between "needs" as identified by a central authority and "demands" as registered by the local community. The question that then arises is: whose preferences (or assessment of preferences) should define the metric for the evaluation? Heterogenous preference orderings almost certainly ensure that different communities will select different combinations of investments. Moreover, none of these need correspond with the center's assessment of the desirable combination.

Because the objective is to empower the poor, their views should play an important role in the evaluation. However, the views of the central authorities also should be considered. First, they may have access to important information (for example, an assessment of the economy's long-run development, a factor that influences the returns to investment in education) that is not incorporated in community-level decision making. Second, the central authorities may be concerned about extra-community impacts, whether positive or negative, or about inequities across regions, neither of which may enter an individual community's decision making. Third, society's willingness to be taxed depends at least to some extent on the people's assessment of the usefulness of the purposes to which tax revenues are put. For this reason alone, it is desirable to have some assessment of impact across all communities against performance measures that society as a whole regards as important—such as student performance, health status, incomes. The outcome of this evaluation then will have to be weighed against those reflecting the preferences of local communities, with some accommodation made between the two.

The Counterfactual

One possible reason why evaluation is not frequently used, and why many evaluations are judged wanting, is the difficulty of the task. To be of value to the policy maker, an evaluation must assess the impact of an intervention relative to what would have happened in the absence of the intervention. Because this alternative outcome cannot be observed, the evaluator must resort to some other technique to identify the counterfactual against which program impact is to be measured. Analytically, the logic of the counterfactual is clear. Identifying the counterfactual empirically is more problematic.

This section first establishes the importance of specifying the counterfactual as accurately as possible. It then compares the main approaches that have been used in practice. Finally, it discusses how beneficiary assessments, an increasingly popular technique used in poverty alleviation programs, can be used as part of a rigorous evaluation.

Specifying the Counterfactual. Three evaluations of Maharashtra's famous Employment Guarantee Scheme (EGS) illustrate the importance of the counterfactual. Introduced in the mid 1970s, EGS was designed to provide employment in small-scale, rural public works projects, such as roads and irrigation facilities. EGS offered guaranteed employment—anyone requesting employment would be employed—but it was designed primarily to target the poor. This was achieved through a self-selecting mechanism that set wages at a level that was likely to attract only the poor. Available evidence suggests that the scheme was successful in providing substantial amounts of employment—around 100 million person-days a year—and was apparently successful in targeting the poor.

To evaluate this project, it would be useful to know the net transfer to the poor. The simplest way of specifying the counterfactual to answer this question is to assume that in the absence of the program the poor would have earned nothing. In this case, the net transfer equals the wage paid by the scheme. This simplistic approach is used often, but it is invariably incorrect and usually leads to overestimated program benefits.

In this particular case, the participants would almost certainly have earned something in the absence of the program. The question is: how much? An alternative but slightly more demanding way of specifying the counterfactual is to assume that in the absence of the program participants would have earned as much as those who did not have access to the scheme. Following this approach, a comparison of mean incomes in two samples of landless and marginal farmers—one containing participants in EGS and the other from an area where the scheme was inoperative—suggests forgone incomes in the range of 50 percent of the wage paid by EGS (Ravallion and Datt, forthcoming).

Yet a third, even more demanding, approach draws on the socioeconomic and demographic characteristics of the participating group itself to predict econometrically what the group would have earned in the absence of the program. Using this approach, a careful econometric investigation of time allocation in two villages suggests that forgone incomes were not large relative to the earnings from participation in the scheme—about 28 percent for men and 10 percent for women (Ravallion and Datt, forthcoming).

As this discussion reveals, choice of the counterfactual will essentially determine the outcome of the evaluation. In the preceding example the three methods arrive at estimates of the net transfer ranging from 100 to 50 percent of the wage paid by the scheme. Hence, a mistake at this point is crucial. The next subsection describes the main evaluation approaches and assesses their relative strengths and weaknesses.

Experimental and Quasi-Experimental Approaches. Two broad categories of evaluation technique can be identified: experimental and quasi-experimental. The experimental approach uses random assignment to place individuals or communities in a "treatment" group (those who will enter the program) or in a "control" group (those who will define the counterfactual). Although this approach has not been widely used, it has been successfully applied in a few instances.

One such case is the Radio Mathematics Project in Nicaragua. The key design feature of this approach was that all eligible schools (schools with at least fifteen grade 1 students) in the four participating provinces had an equal chance of being placed in the treatment group or in the control group. During the period of implementation (1976–1978), students in both groups were administered mathematics tests. Test results formed the basis on which it was concluded that the performance of those receiving the radio education program was statistically better than that of those in the control group (Newman, Rawlings, and Gertler, 1994). Because the process of random assignment ensured that the two groups were statistically equivalent in all respects, differences in performance could be confidently attributed to the radio program. It is this characteristic of the approach—its ability to arrive at convincing results—that makes it so attractive. Without the statistical equivalence, differences in performance may reflect differential access to the program or differences between the groups.

An alternative approach uses quasi-experimental techniques to determine what would have happened in the absence of the program. Here the counterfactual is inferred either from the pre-program behavior of participants (reflexive comparison) or from the behavior of a "matched" group whose members do not receive program services. The preceding discussion of the EGS illustrates both techniques.

Research in the United States comparing experimental and quasi-experimental approaches has generally found that the latter cannot replicate the results of the former. A recent survey (Grossman, 1994) indicates that current consensus considers random assignment to be the evaluation technique that produces the most defensible results. For some situations, however, this approach is infeasible—for example, when the program is so large relative to the rest of the economy that it can have general equilibrium effects that touch all members of society. Changes in the wage rate as a result of ESF in Bolivia are one such case. Here econometric estimation will almost certainly be required. Another example occurs when the intervention is designed to reach all members of society. Phasing possibilities aside, the introduction of a program nationwide precludes the possibility of establishing a control group. In such a case, other techniques, such as quasi-experimental methods, will be required. Difficulties also can arise when the program is small relative to the rest of the economy, as in the case of a small pilot. Although groups can be randomly assigned in such a case, the results of the study cannot always be assumed to hold for the population as a whole because of scale effects.

Beneficiary Assessment. Beneficiary assessment is increasingly recognized as a useful tool for conveying and eliciting information. The method typically involves participant observation and intensive interviewing. "The term *beneficiary assessment* is used for participant observation, qualitative interviewing, and related techniques to gauge beneficiary values and preferences at any point in the project cycle" (Salmen, 1989). Thus the approach can elicit information on many factors at the household and community levels that more quantitative techniques cannot. But the issue of interest in this chapter is whether beneficiary assessment can constitute or contribute to rigorous evaluation of poverty alleviation programs.

Consider the following example drawn from a review (Salmen, 1989) of twelve projects in which beneficiary assessments were carried out. Salmen (1989) notes that the most general and basic need in the projects revealed by the assessments was for better communication between project staff and beneficiaries. In one case 50 percent of the people who were to be resettled as part of the Recife Metropolitan Development Project did not know where they would be moved. Following the assessment project, management decided to distribute leaflets door-to-door and hold group meetings to correct the situation.

Thus, the process led to a change in the implementation of the project, but that did not constitute an evaluation of impact. Without doubt, beneficiary assessments generate valuable information on the participants' view of project success. However, to constitute an evaluation that information would have to be used in the context of either an experimental or quasi-experimental evaluation in order to arrive at a genuine measure of impact relative to a well-specified counterfactual. Such an approach provides an evaluation from the perspective of participants, but to be convincing it would almost certainly require larger and more carefully selected samples than have been used to date.

Incentives and Institutions

Evaluation often conjures up a picture of efforts to assess the relationship between inputs subject to control by the implementing agency and outputs intended to approximate the ultimate objective of improving the living standards of the poor. But an exclusive focus on input-output relationships is at best partial and could be misleading. In all dimensions of economic analysis, increasing attention is being given to the institutions and incentives governing the implementation of policies and programs. Thus, looking at different combinations of incentives and institutions with the same basic inputs may be as important as looking at different quantities and combinations of inputs with the same incentives and institutions. In this context, the term "incentives and institutions" embraces both formal rules and regulations, such as economy-wide policies and within-program controls and structures, and informal ones, such as social conventions and local power relationships.

A striking example of this point comes from the experience of evaluations in education. A study of Egyptian primary schools found that, after controlling for initial levels of student achievement and parental education, the variation in improvement in student achievement during a given year was very large, and of that variation only 16 percent could be explained by differences in measured attributes of teachers and schools (Hanushek and Lavy, 1994). Other process- or performance-related factors were apparently playing a major role.

Perhaps the key process factor, especially in poverty alleviation programs, is the degree of participation by intended beneficiaries. Participation is claimed to improve project implementation. Evidence on the impact of participation on project implementation is growing rapidly but is mainly in the form of case studies, although a recent econometric study of 121 rural water supply projects confirms that participation improves overall project performance (Isham, Narayan, and Pritchett, 1994). The purpose of this chapter, however, is not to offer a view on the merits of participation, but to comment on the implications of participation for evaluation.

Participation can take different forms and occur at different stages: the design stage, during construction, during implementation, or at all these stages. Participation can range from minimal consultation to participant control over key decisions. The environment for participation can vary because of at least two factors. The first concerns social structure. For example, participation may be more effective in relatively homogeneous communities; it may be less effective where a minority group has sufficient power to capture the decision making process or where a minority group is systematically excluded. The second concerns the characteristics of the proposed intervention. For example, within-community participation may be a less important consideration in a project that has significant spillover effects to other communities, or that has impact on only a small segment of the community, than one for which the benefits are evenly distributed throughout the community.

The basic point is that the degree and mode of participation are design variables: they can be varied to fit particular communities and particular projects. This then suggests the role of evaluation. Program sponsors would like to know where and in what form participation is most effective. A school decentralization project in Peru illustrates the general point. The experiment entails comparing different degrees of decentralization and parental participation in decisions on school management dealing with budget, personnel, pedagogy, and internal administration. One variant would leave decision making in these areas in the hands of the existing intermediary organization, the local office in charge of management and financial decision making for schools under its jurisdiction. A second variant would assign decision making authority for everything except personnel to the school director with the school council, which includes representatives from parents' groups, acting in an advisory capacity. A third variant would increase the school council's role to include voting rights on both the annual budget and the medium-term institutional development plan.

The project contains an evaluation component designed to test the impact of the different degrees of decentralization and participation on educational outcomes as measured by student performance and teaching practices and on the efficiency of school management as measured by unit costs and other indicators. The experimental design of the evaluation—interventions will be randomly assigned—ensures that firm conclusions can be drawn about the future development of the program. More such exercises that deal with a variety of participatory alternatives should be high on the program sponsors' list of priorities for future work.

Similarly, a convincing demonstration of the impact of beneficiary assessments would be helpful. A simple comparison of the differences in outcomes of projects with beneficiary assessments and those without would not be satisfactory because the samples would almost certainly not be random and would not control for the depth and duration of beneficiary assessments. An experiment involving random assignment would allow a convincing evaluation of impact but may be difficult to implement. A more suitable research strategy in this situation would be to replicate the approach used in the study of participation in the water supply projects mentioned earlier. Project outcomes could be regressed on a range of control variables and on measures of the intensity and frequency of beneficiary assessments. Such a study could help identify projects for which the assessments are likely to be most valuable and measure the return from repeated assessments.

What to Evaluate

Because budgets allocated to evaluation will probably remain small in the foreseeable future, it is important to allocate scarce evaluation resources as effectively as possible.

First, beneficiary assessments and similar diagnostic tools have a potentially important role in improving the effectiveness of project implementation. Whether evaluators are yet in a position to provide convincing evidence on the costs and benefits of these tools and hence on whether more resources should be allocated to such activities is an open question. Research along the lines suggested above would take us beyond case histories and provide a firmer foundation for future development of the approach. To this end, it would be useful to start assembling a database of projects using beneficiary assessments that could eventually be used in a statistical investigation of their impact. Beneficiary assessments and similar diagnostic tools can be used to elucidate and expand the results of quantitative evaluations—a quantitative evaluation may establish project success or failure but not explain why.

Second, the use of more intensive techniques, both experimental and quasi-experimental, designed to provide a firmer statistical base for evaluation needs to be carefully justified. Several criteria can be formulated around the basic proposition that the expected benefits of the evaluation must exceed its costs. In particular, officials might want to concentrate on interventions for cases in which the outcome is very uncertain, the program is highly innovative, and the costs of implementing an inferior design, due to inadequate awareness or acceptance of a superior design, are large (Dennis and Borouch, 1989).

Third, the choice between experimental and quasi-experimental methods needs to be considered. The consensus is in favor of experimental techniques where they are feasible, but, as discussed earlier, they are not always feasible. General equilibrium effects, national coverage, and ethical considerations are among the reasons that render random assignment either infeasible or undesirable.

Finally, evaluations have some of the characteristics of an international public good in that their results can be appropriated by others at no cost. The Nicaraguan Radio Mathematics Project illustrates the point well. Its results benefitted many other countries besides Nicaragua. Activities that produce benefits for those other than the investing party tend to be underfunded, as is the case with evaluation. To offset this cause of worldwide underinvestment in evaluation, donor agencies should take advantage of their involvement in many innovative projects throughout the developing world by building careful evaluations into these projects. Indeed the World Bank is already implementing this idea in several projects, including the Peru School Decentralization Project discussed above. Such actions can offset the worldwide tendency to underinvest in evaluation and significantly increase the international return to project innovation.

References

Coa, R. *Impact Evaluation Design for Social Investment Fund Intervention.* La Paz, Bolivia: Institutional Development Division, Social Investment Fund, 1992.

Dennis, M., and Borouch, R. F. "Randomized Experiments for Planning and Testing Projects in Developing Countries: Threshold Conditions." *Evaluation Review,* 1989, 12 (1), 292–309.

Grossman, J. B. "Evaluating Social Policies: Principles and U.S. Experience." *World Bank Research Observer,* 1994, 9 (2), 159–180.

Hanushek, E. A., and Lavy, V. *School Quality, Achievement Bias, and Dropout Behavior in Egypt.* Living Standards Measurement Study Working Paper 107. Washington, D.C.: World Bank, 1994.

Isham, J., Narayan, D., and Pritchett, L. *Does Participation Improve Project Performance? Establishing Causality with Subjective Data.* World Bank Policy Research Working Paper no. 1357. Washington, D.C.: World Bank, 1994.

Newman, J., Jorgensen, S., and Pradhan, M. "How Did Workers Benefit from Bolivia's Emergency Social Fund?" *World Bank Economic Review,* 1991, 5 (2), 367–393.

Newman, J., Rawlings, L., and Gertler, P. "Using Randomized Control Designs in Evaluating Social Sector Programs in Developing Countries." *World Bank Research Observer,* 1994, 9 (2), 181–202.

Ravallion, M., and Datt, G. "Is Targeting Through a Work Requirement Efficient? Some Evidence for Rural India." In D. van de Walle and K. Nead (eds.), *Public Spending and the Poor: Theory and Evidence.* Baltimore, Md.: Johns Hopkins University Press for the World Bank (forthcoming).

Salmen, L. F. "Beneficiary Assessment: Improving the Design and Implementation of Development Projects." *Evaluation Review,* 1989, 13 (3).

Valadez, J., and Bamberger, M. *Monitoring and Evaluating Social Programs in Developing Countries: A Handbook for Policy Makers, Managers, and Researchers.* Development Studies Series, the World Bank Economic Development Institute (forthcoming).

World Bank. *Staff Appraisal Report: Bolivia: Social Investment Fund Project.* Human Resources Division, Country Department III: Latin American and the Caribbean Regional Office. Washington, D.C.: World Bank, 1990a, 11.

World Bank. *World Development Report 1990: Poverty.* New York: Oxford University Press, 1990b.

World Bank. *Staff Appraisal Report: Mexico: Second Decentralization and Regional Development Project.* Natural Resources Management and Rural Poverty Operations Division; Country Department II: Latin America and the Caribbean Regional Office. Washington, D.C.: World Bank, 1994.

LYN SQUIRE is director of the Policy Research Department, Development Economics Vice Presidency of the World Bank.

This chapter presents a macroeconomic framework for evaluating the effects of policy-based adjustment programs, with an illustration from a recent World Bank evaluation.

A Framework for Evaluating Policy Adjustment Programs: Lessons from a Cross-Country Evaluation

William H. Branson, Carl Jayarajah

We developed the macroeconomic framework presented in this chapter during the course of our work in evaluating World Bank structural and sectoral adjustment loans. When we began our work in the mid 1980s, no agreed framework for assessing the macroeconomic component of such loans existed. Gradually a framework was developed, first for use in country loan evaluations and more recently for cross-country comparative overviews.

The framework is designed for situations in which an estimated model of the economy is not available, such as when a country is considering mid-course correction, or for cross-country evaluations of countries with differing structures and data gaps. It is basically a version of Robert Mundell's (1962) policy assignment model, which assigns policy instruments to targets following the principle of comparative advantage. An analysis of debt sustainability is added to include an intertemporal dimension.

Although the framework can be applied to both country and cross-country studies, this chapter focuses on a cross-country application. We begin with a discussion of the assignment model and illustrate its use with an example from a recent evaluation of World Bank structural and sectoral adjustment lending (World Bank, Operations Evaluation Department, forthcoming). The example, which draws from World Bank experience in adjustment lending in fifty-five countries, strongly suggests that when a macro framework is introduced early in the design of an economic adjustment program and decisions on policy are guided by the framework, the policy instruments are more likely to have their intended impact and their results are more likely to be sustainable.

NEW DIRECTIONS FOR EVALUATION, no. 67, Fall 1995 © Jossey-Bass Publishers

The Assignment Model

A well-designed economic adjustment program has realistic objectives for internal balance, represented by growth in gross domestic product (GDP) and inflation; external balance, represented by foreign exchange reserves; and the current account (and thereby growth of debt). The program sets the instruments for fiscal policy, monetary policy, and the exchange rate, which are expected simultaneously to bring the economy close to the objectives. No issue of policy assignment arises at this stage.

During the course of the program, unpredictable disturbances almost always appear, and policy has to be adjusted. With enough time and information, all policy instruments are adjusted and the program redesigned. If time and information are in short supply, knowing which instrument should take the lead in adjustment—depending on which target variable has gone off course—can be essential. The reason is that some pairings of instruments to targets will lead to convergence back toward the joint objectives, whereas other pairings will lead away from the objectives. The first pairings are *stable* policy assignments; the second are *unstable*.

The assignment problem is illustrated in a two-variable case with a fixed exchange rate in Figure 2.1. There the policy variables are the interest rate, R, and the budget surplus, S. These are used for ease of illustration. We could use the controllable part of the money supply and the full-resource-employment surplus, if they were measurable. Here we cut through the complexities involved in using strictly controllable instruments by assuming that the program has targets for the interest rate and the surplus.

A program is assumed to set values for these to maintain internal balance, along the II line, and external balance, along the EE line, simultaneously, at point T. Internal balance might be defined as satisfactory noninflationary growth, and external balance as a satisfactory balance of payments. Both equilibrium lines have negative slopes. To maintain internal balance if the budget surplus is reduced, interest rates must be raised. Similarly for external balance, a reduction in the budget surplus stimulates demand and reduces the current account surplus. This requires an increase in interest rates to maintain balance-of-payments equilibrium. The EE line is flatter than II because interest rates influence the capital account, as well as demand. If the economy is very small, has an excellent credit rating, and has an open capital account, the EE line could become nearly horizontal at the London Interbank Offered Rate of interest (LIBOR) plus the country risk premium over that rate.

A program implicitly attempts to estimate where the II and EE lines are, and sets the two policy instruments to hit the simultaneous target point T. At this point no question of policy assignment arises. However, consider what happens if an unanticipated shock throws the economy out of equilibrium. As an example, suppose the economy is at point A in Figure 2.1, with balance-of-payments equilibrium but inflation developing. Assignment of fiscal policy to maintain internal balance would move the policy point to B, with a balance-

Figure 2.1. The Assignment Problem

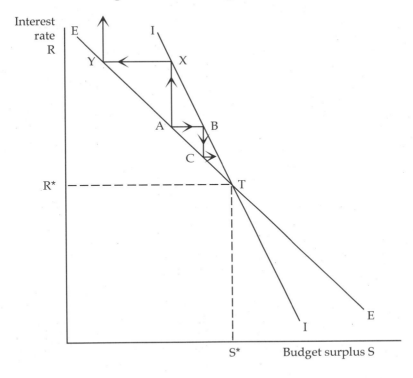

of-payments surplus. Assignment of monetary policy to maintain external balance moves the policy point to C, and so on. This assignment is clearly converging to the equilibrium target point T.

On the other hand, assignment of monetary policy to restore internal balance would move the policy point to X, with interest rates rising to dampen aggregate demand. This would yield a surplus on the balance of payments and a reserve accumulation. If fiscal policy were assigned to external balance, movement would be toward point Y—clearly an unstable assignment. If fiscal policy had no assignment, the balance-of-payments surplus would tempt the spending ministries in the government to argue for easier fiscal policy. This situation, at a point such as X, is similar to one observed during the investment boom in Indonesia in 1991. The arguments then were that further fiscal tightening was unnecessary because monetary policy had dealt with the demand problem and the reserve position was satisfactory.

The application of the assignment model to the evaluation of structural adjustment programs uses the principle of comparative advantage to assign fiscal policy to internal balance, the real exchange rate to the current account, and monetary policy to external balance in terms of foreign exchange reserves.

In the use of this framework we assume that an unacceptably high rate of inflation indicates the need to reduce the primary (or noninterest) budget deficit or increase the surplus. This can be interpreted as reducing inflation by reducing aggregate demand, or it can be interpreted as reducing the need for inflation tax financing of the deficit.

The two objectives for external balance are appropriate levels of the current account or resource balance and of foreign exchange reserves. None of the countries studied has a purely floating exchange rate. Most of them have adopted what is called in the World Bank a "flexible" or "realistic" exchange rate policy. Generally, this means moving the nominal exchange rate to prevent appreciation of the currency in real terms, or even to generate some gradual real depreciation. The objective is to limit the deficit on current account. Thus the path of the real exchange rate is tied to the current account objective. Then the domestic rate of inflation gives the path of the nominal exchange rate that is consistent with the targeted path of the real rate.

Most countries have some degree of international capital mobility, so that if their real interest rates get too far below international rates, there will be capital outflow and loss of reserves. This implies that maintaining external balance in the level of foreign exchange reserves requires keeping real interest rates high enough, relative to international rates, to induce investors to keep their deposits and other investments in the country. Thus, monetary policy must manage the mix of financing for the deficit such that domestic real interest rates are at least as high as world rates, plus any expected rate of real depreciation of the home currency, plus whatever risk premium exists on local assets.

Debt Sustainability

The intertemporal consistency of the application of the macro framework in any given case can be checked by looking at the arithmetic of the government budget constraint in the analysis of debt sustainability that is currently used in the World Bank (illustrated by Anand and Wijnbergen, 1989). The government's budget constraint in real terms can be written as a formula for the growth of the ratio of debt to GDP:

(1) $db = (r - n)b + p - s$

where b is the ratio of debt to GDP, db is its arithmetic (not percentage) annual growth, r is the real interest rate, n is the growth rate of real GDP, p is the primary deficit as a fraction of GDP, and s is the ratio of seigniorage to GDP. Seigniorage here includes both the inflation tax and real growth in demand for base money as the economy grows.

The intertemporal consistency of the application of the macro framework could be checked as follows, at least in principle. Seigniorage s would be determined from the projected growth rate and inflation objective, combined with an estimate of the velocity of base money. The interest rate would come from the external balance requirement, given the outstanding stock of debt that establishes the risk premium. In general, the central bank knows approximately what rate is needed to prevent excessive capital outflow. The rate of growth of debt that is consistent with the interest rate objective would be calculated from the growth rate of wealth of the relevant lending population to give the permissible *db* consistent with external balance. The debt dynamics equation (1) would then yield the value of the primary deficit *p* that is consistent with internal balance. This check also can be interpreted as a check of the sustainability of the debt path, given the primary deficit *p*.

In some cases, estimates of the velocity of base money and its sensitivity to changing interest rates or inflation expectations, or of the relation between increasing debt issue and interest rates, may be unavailable or unreliable. In these cases, policy must proceed incrementally. The directions for policy change indicated by the debt sustainability approach are the same as those indicated by the assignment model. If inflation is unacceptably high, reduce the primary deficit. If the current account deficit is too large, devalue in real terms. If foreign exchange reserves are too low or falling too fast, tighten monetary policy, that is, shift from money financing to debt financing of the existing deficit. These three relationships give the direction of policy actions and the expected outcomes.

Applying the Framework

We recently completed an evaluation of World Bank structural and sectoral adjustment lending (World Bank, Operations Evaluation Department, forthcoming) in which we applied this framework to a sample of fifty-five countries in which the World Bank had completed 146 adjustment loans. This chapter outlines the results to illustrate how the framework was applied. The evaluation method was basically cross-country before and after an adjustment period, as defined by the timing of the loans. For each country we established an adjustment period, generally from the beginning of the first loan to a year after the final disbursement.

Policy Adjustments and Outcomes. The macroeconomic framework was used to establish the normal direction for change in each policy instrument, that is, the "right" policy, and the expected outcome, that is, the "right" result, for the associated target, all in qualitative terms. The sample countries were then compared across their adjustment periods and sorted into four categories, with results shown in Table 2.1.

The first category, comprising the majority, shows the number of countries that followed the right policy and got the right result—the "normal" group or the "good" cases, totalling 100 out of 150 cases. The other three categories are the "abnormal" ones. The second category, the "bad" cases, shows the number of countries that followed the wrong policy and got the wrong result—consistent with the framework. The last two categories, the "ugly" cases, cover countries with results contrary to the macro framework. Countries in the third

Table 2.1. Policies and Results in the Sample Countries

Category	Internal Balance (Reduce fiscal deficit ---> decreased inflation)	Resource Balance (Real devaluation ---> increased resource balance)	External Balance (Reduce negative interest differential ---> increased net foreign exchange reserves)
Right policy Right outcome	27	39	32
Wrong policy Wrong outcome	10	2	8
Right policy Wrong outcome	9	3	7
Wrong policy Right outcome	7	4	1

Note: The values represent the number of countries. Column totals are unequal because of absence of data for some policy areas in several countries.
Source: OED estimates

category followed the right policy but got the wrong result—presumably because they experienced unanticipated negative exogenous shocks, such as a reduction in inward transfers or a deterioration of the terms of trade. Countries in the last category were lucky: they followed the wrong policy but got the right result. They experienced unanticipated favorable exogenous events. Because some countries are in more than one of the last three categories, thirty-one countries are in at least one of the abnormal categories. They are listed in Table 2.2.

Of the nineteen countries in the "unlucky" category—right policy, but wrong outcomes—only Madagascar appears twice. None of the countries had bad luck across the board. Thus there seems to be little correlation across the adjustment areas of the events that caused the wrong outcomes. The same is true of the "lucky" countries—right outcomes even with wrong policies— among which only Côte d'Ivoire appears twice. The lack of correlation across policy areas of cases with seemingly perverse results permits us to discuss these cases by policy area.

Some correlation exists across policy areas where wrong policy choices predictably led to bad results (see Table 2.2). Nicaragua and Sudan have checks across all three columns marked WW (wrong policy, wrong results); Bolivia and Guyana have checks across two. Several of the countries in this row have suffered from some form of social unrest or even war during the period of attempted adjustment.

Table 2.2. Policies and Results in Selected Adjusting Countries

Country	Adjustment Period	Internal			Resource			External		
		WW	WR	RW	WW	WR	RW	WW	WR	RW
Argentina	1985–			•				•		
Bolivia	1980–81	•				•		•		
Brazil	1983–85	•				•				•
Burundi	1986–		•							
Colombia	1985–89	•								
Congo	1987–89		•							•
Costa Rica	1982–89			•						
Côte d'Ivoire	1980–87		•			•				•
Ecuador	1984–89			•						
Gambia, The	1986–87					•				
Ghana	1983–88						•			
Guyana	1980–84	•						•		
Hungary	1984–91			•				•		
Kenya	1980–84								•	
Madagascar	1984–			•						•
Mexico	1983–									•
Nepal	1987–88		•							
Nicaragua	1980–85	•			•			•		
Niger	1986–90		•							
Nigeria	1983–86	•								
Pakistan	1982–83		•							•
Paraguay	1980–86			•						
Philippines	1980–84		•							•
Sudan	1980–86	•			•			•		
Tanzania[a]	1981–83			•				•		
Togo	1983–						•			
Turkey	1980–85	•								
Uruguay	1984–			•						
Zaire	1983–88			•						
Zambia	1985–88	•					•			
Zimbabwe	1983–86	•								
Total		10	7	9	2	4	3	7	1	7

Note: WW=wrong policy and wrong outcome; WR=wrong policy and right outcome; RW=right policy and wrong outcome.

[a] Tanzania undertook a further adjustment program in 1986; that experience has not yet been reviewed by OED.

Source: OED estimates

Debt Sustainability. The debt sustainability of the sample countries was analyzed by studying the components of equation (1), which gives the change in the ratio of debt to GDP. All of the adjusting countries are international borrowers, so their b terms, the debt/GDP ratios, are positive. Thus the sign of the growth term ($r - n$) will determine whether the debt process is itself unstable. If ($r - n$) is positive, the debt ratio will tend to be growing by feeding on itself; the country is borrowing to service its debt. In this case, for the overall process to be stable, that is for db to be negative, the primary deficit less seigniorage term ($p - s$) would have to be negative. If the growth term is negative, the primary deficit less seigniorage term could be zero or even slightly positive. The country could grow out of its debt burden.

An unsustainable debt situation can be improved by changing some combination of four variables in equation (1): the stock of debt, the interest rate, the growth rate, or the primary deficit. Restructuring can reduce interest rates or the stock of debt. Low-income countries can reduce interest rates by concessional borrowing. Most of the countries with sustainable debt burdens substantially reduced the primary deficit as part of the adjustment program, as shown in Table 2.1.

The components of the right-hand side of equation (1) were calculated for each of the sample countries for the three periods: preadjustment, adjustment, and postadjustment. The calculations use period averages for n, b, p, and s for each country. The choice of data to use for the real borrowing rate r is more problematic. Most of the adjusting countries had tightly controlled financial markets and negative real interest rates, measured in domestic currency, before adjustment. After the adjustment period, most had liberalized their financial markets to some extent and raised real interest rates. However, for many countries the measured real rate even after adjustment is not completely market determined and does not show the true cost to the country of borrowing.

We have used projected interest payments for 1994 (World Bank, 1993) as a fraction of end-1993 debt, less average U.S. inflation for 1988–1992, as the real borrowing rate for each country in the postadjustment period. Compared with a real LIBOR of perhaps 5 percent, this calculation yields an average real rate of about 0.5 percent for all forty adjustors for which we have data, and -0.5 percent for the sub-Saharan countries. This calculation makes almost all of the growth factors negative.

Of the forty countries (out of fifty) for which we have postadjustment data, twenty have a sustainable debt path—that is, the change in the debt/GDP ratio db is negative—in the postadjustment period. This leaves thirteen, or 32.5 percent of the adjusters, with db positive—that is, a rising debt/GDP ratio (see Table 2.3).

The first two columns in Table 2.3 show postadjustment growth factors and ($p - s$) terms. A positive entry in either of these two columns warns of an unsustainable debt path. The estimated annual change in debt/GDP ratios, in the absence of additional concessional finance or rescheduling, is the sum of

Table 2.3. Countries with Unsustainable Debt Paths in the Postadjustment Period

Countries	Growth Factor $(r - n)\,b$	Primary Deficit Less Seigniorage[a] $(p - s)$	Annual Increase in Debt/GDP Ratio (db)	Change in Debt/GDP Across Adjustment Period[b]
Low-Income Countries				
Bangladesh	-3.2	6.1	2.9	14.3
Guyana	-10.2	13.6	3.4	190.5
Nepal	-2.1	5.5	3.4	14.6
Pakistan	-2.8	4.4	1.6	0.5
Middle-Income Countries				
Nicaragua	8.2	-0.9	7.3	134.4
Sub-Saharan Countries				
Central African Republic	-0.3	2.5	2.2	23.7
Congo	0.2	6.7	6.9	-79.0
Côte d'Ivoire	4.1	11.1	15.2	79.1
Guinea-Bissau	0.0	1.6	1.5	195.3
Niger	-1.3	6.9	5.6	-9.2
Sudan	-2.4	12.8	10.4	12.7
Zambia	0.5	7.1	7.6	12.4
Zimbabwe	-1.0	6.1	5.1	25.0

[a]Seigniorage is defined as the change in the central bank's claims on the public sector (IFS Lines 12a, 12b, 12bx, and 12c) as a percentage of GDP.

[b]The change in debt/GDP is the difference between the first year of the postadjustment period and the last year of the preadjustment period.

Source: OED estimates

the entries in these two columns, shown in the third column. The last column shows the actual change in the debt/GDP ratio across the adjustment period; this is the ratio in the first year after the adjustment period less the ratio in the last year before it. In Congo and Niger, the two countries with negative entries in the last column, the ratio was reduced as part of the adjustment, by debt forgiveness or rescheduling. However in the postadjustment period in these countries the ratio is again rising.

Countries with a negative growth factor (the majority listed in Table 2.3) do not have a debt path that is inherently unsustainable. Of the thirteen countries, only four—Congo, Côte d'Ivoire, Nicaragua, and Zambia—have positive growth factors, and those of Congo and Zambia are very small. Thus for most of the countries in Table 2.3, the problem is not an interest burden that is out of control. Their debt ratios are rising due to the current primary deficit. If they were to reduce this deficit to make $(p - s)$ zero, the path would become stable. Of the nine countries with negative growth factors, Sudan and Zimbabwe have such large primary deficits that their debt to GDP ratios are growing by more than five percentage points a year. All of the countries with positive growth factors have debt to GDP ratios growing by more than five percentage points a year. Given the growth factor, the third column in Table 2.3 indicates how much the primary deficit would have to be reduced to stop the growth in the debt/GDP ratio. The seven countries with entries above 5 percent seem to face serious debt problems after adjustment.

Investment, Adjustment Policy, and Growth. An adjustment period is almost inevitably a period of heightened uncertainty in the economy, particularly for investors. Policy changes are imminent, but their precise direction, extent, and permanence are not known. To forestall opposition, the government may proceed in steps, without fully revealing all the intended policy changes. In such a situation a rational investor may wait until some of the uncertainty is resolved, so an investment pause is to be expected during the adjustment period.

The investment pause is apparent in the data from the fifty-five sample countries. In thirty-seven of the countries, mostly in Latin America and sub-Saharan Africa, the investment/GDP ratio fell during the adjustment period. In ten of the thirty-seven countries, investment began to recover after adjustment; for several others, it is too soon to tell. The downward trend in investment was most marked in the sub-Saharan Africa countries. The average investment to GDP ratio, which had fallen in the adjustment period, generally declined further in the postadjustment period. The investment to GDP ratio started to recover in the postadjustment period in five of the countries in the group in which the investment ratio had fallen during adjustment.

As widely noted, normal positive relations between investment and growth can break down during an adjustment period. At new effective prices, old capital could become obsolete, reducing the average product of capital. The marginal product of appropriate new investment could rise, but investment could fail to respond because of uncertainty. The adjustment program could stimulate an increase in capacity utilization in positively affected sectors. Thus, a fall in investment could be associated with continued growth in output, supported by the adjustment loan itself. This would tend to suppress the normal positive relationship between investment and growth during the adjustment period, even though the adjustment itself is aimed at strengthening this relationship in the long run.

Table 2.4 summarizes the results of a regression of average per capita GDP growth rates on the average ratio of total fixed investment to GDP, where the averages are over time for each country and the regressions are run across countries. The regressions are estimated separately for the three periods, and for three subsets of adjusters, as well as the entire sample. The estimation is by ordinary least squares. The coefficients of the investment ratio can be interpreted as cross-country marginal products of capital with a common production function for GDP.

The estimates of the investment coefficients in Table 2.4 are significantly positive for the entire sample and for the middle-income countries in the pre- and postadjustment periods. The investment coefficient is marginally significant for the sub-Saharan Africa countries in the preadjustment period but not in the postadjustment period. This is consistent with the slow recovery of investment in sub-Saharan Africa after adjustment. The investment coefficients are completely insignificant for all groups in the adjustment period, as expected. The coefficients for the entire sample and for the middle-income countries rise from pre- to postadjustment period, consistent with effective adjustment.

The changes in policy variables in Table 2.1 are added to the growth equation in Table 2.5. Since a stable investment-growth relationship exists in the postadjustment period, we focus on the effects of changes in policy variables from the pre- to the postadjustment period on the growth rate of real per capita GDP in the postadjustment period. Thus the added policy variables in Table 2.5 are the change in the ratio of the fiscal balance to GDP, the fiscal deficit (FD, an increase reflects a reduction of the deficit), the percentage change in the real effective exchange rate (REER, an increase is an appreciation of the home currency), and the change in the real interest differential (RID) all measured as postadjustment less preadjustment. The top panel in Table 2.5 shows results for all the sample countries for which we have a full data set; the bottom panel breaks the sample by country type.

Equation (1) in Table 2.5 shows the results of adding the change in all three policy variables to the postadjustment growth regression, run across the thirty-two countries for which we have sufficient postadjustment data on all variables. The investment ratio remains significantly positive. All three policy changes contribute positively to postadjustment growth, with the reduction in the fiscal deficit and the real depreciation statistically significant. Thus the "right policies" shown in Table 2.1 also increase the growth rate.

The change in the real interest differential is insignificant in this equation. This is not surprising. In the short run, the change is aimed at foreign exchange

Table 2.4. Coefficients of Gross Domestic Investment as Percentage of GDP in Basic Growth Equation

Country Group	Number of Observations	Preadjustment GDI/GDP	Preadjustment Adjusted R²	Adjustment GDI/GDP	Adjustment Adjusted R²	Postadjustment GDI/GDP	Postadjustment Adjusted R²
All	53	0.10 (2.6)	0.09	0.07 (1.3)	0.01	0.17 (2.4)	0.11
Low-income	5	0.50 (0.58)	-0.15	0.08 (0.4)	-0.19	0.09 (0.8)	-0.09
Middle-income	22	0.24 (2.5)	0.20	0.04 (0.4)	-0.03	0.40 (3.9)	0.48
Sub-Saharan	25	0.06 (1.5)	0.05	0.00 (0.0)	-0.04	-0.01 (0.1)	-0.06

Note: Dependent variable: real per capita growth, Y/P. Equation: percent change (Y/P = a0 + a1(I/Y) + e. Numbers in parentheses are absolute values of t statistics.

Source: OED estimates

Table 2.5. Macro Policies and Growth

| Country Group | Number of Observations | GDI/GDP | Change in | | | Adjusted R^2 |
			FD	REER	RID	
(1) All	32	0.26 (4.24)	0.18 (2.76)	-0.01 (2.15)	0.01 (0.80)	0.55
(2) All	32	0.26 (4.29)	0.18 (2.83)	-0.01 (2.72)		0.56
(3) All	36	0.27 (4.44)	0.12 (1.87)	-0.01 (2.63)		0.49
(4) Low- and middle-income	19	0.25	0.14	-0.01		0.78
(5) Middle-income	15	0.34 (4.66)	0.17 (0.88)	-0.01 (2.84)		0.84
(6) Sub-Saharan	13	-0.02 (0.09)	0.60 (2.36)	0.01 (0.24)		0.29

Note: Dependent variable: real per capita GDP growth in postadjustment period, Y/P. Equation: percent change $(Y/P) = a0 + a1(I/Y) + a2$ (change in REER) + $a3$ (change in FD) + $a4$ (change in RID) + 3.

FD=fiscal deficit; REER=real effective exchange rate; RID=real interest rate differential.

Numbers in parentheses are absolute values of t statistics.

Source: OED estimates

reserves. In the longer run, it will have beneficial effects on growth through the efficiency of capital allocation across sectors. Since the RID was insignificant in all the regressions we estimated, it is eliminated in equation (2), with no change in the results.

Equation (3) adds the four countries that were excluded due to the lack of data on RID. These are Congo, Mauritania, Paraguay, and Zaire. All but Mauritania are perverse cases (among the "ugly") in Table 2.1. Their inclusion weakens the fit of the equation and the fiscal deficit result. However, the impression from Table 2.5 remains clear: the right stabilization policies increase growth in the postadjustment period.

Equation (4) aggregates the low- and middle-income countries. The results are the same as in equation (2), with a large improvement in the fit of the equation. Excluding sub-Saharan Africa improves the fit. Equation (5) includes only the middle-income countries; because we have only four low-income countries, we cannot estimate a meaningful regression for them. With only middle-income countries, the coefficient of the investment ratio increases, and that of the fiscal deficit loses significance. Comparing equations (4) and (5), one can say that investment is more productive in the middle-income countries, but deficit reduction is more certain to contribute to growth in the low-income countries. This impression is reinforced by equation (6), run across sub-Saharan African countries. There, investment and depreciation change sign and become completely insignificant, and the fit is markedly worse than in (4) or (5), but the fiscal coefficient increases dramatically and remains highly significant. In sub-Saharan Africa, only the fiscal part of the package seems to contribute significantly to growth.

Conclusion

We have presented here the current state of the macro framework, based on an assignment model and debt dynamics that introduce explicitly an intertemporal dimension to the evaluation. As shown by our sample, the application of this macro framework would presumably have improved the macro outcomes of the adjustment programs. We saw in Table 2.1 that countries that followed the framework's fiscal recommendation generally experienced a reduction in inflation. We also saw that following policies indicated by the framework improved postadjustment growth. An OED evaluation (World Bank, Operations Evaluation Department, forthcoming) of the social impacts of adjustment indicates that both inflation reduction and faster growth contribute to poverty reduction. Thus an earlier introduction of the macro framework and adherence to its policy indications would on average have improved the effects of the programs in these dimensions.

These findings suggest, as have previous OED evaluations of policy-based lending, that the existence of a macro framework and macro policies consistent with it should be a precondition for an adjustment loan. The framework is most effective if it is developed by the borrower, so that it effectively reflects the borrower's preferences about instruments for adjustment. Thus the existence or development of the macro framework should be a normal part of the adjustment loan conditions attached to adjustment loans and up front among them. Adherence to the macro framework and its policy indicators helps to sustain the results of the adjustment program. Thus any adjustment program should be embedded in a clear macro framework that ensures consistency of policy and stability of policy adjustments. This will improve the probability of recovery and growth after adjustment.

References

Anand, R., and Wijnbergen, S. van. "Inflation and the Financing of Government Expenditure: An Introductory Analysis with an Application to Turkey." *World Bank Economic Review*, Jan. 1989, 3.

Mundell, R. A. "The Appropriate Use of Monetary and Fiscal Policy Under Fixed Exchange Rates." International Monetary Fund *Staff Papers*, 1962, 9 (1).

World Bank. *World Debt Tables, 1993.* Washington, D.C.: World Bank, 1993.

World Bank, Operations Evaluation Department. *Structural and Sectoral Adjustment: World Bank Experience, 1980–1992.* Washington, D.C.: World Bank, forthcoming.

World Bank, Operations Evaluation Department. *The Social Impact of Adjustment.* Washington, D.C.: World Bank, forthcoming.

WILLIAM H. BRANSON is professor of economics at Princeton University.

CARL JAYARAJAH is principal economist, Operations Evaluation Department of the World Bank.

Assessing the quality of public institutions requires analysis of the legal framework that influences the performance, capacity, accountability, and life cycle of government agencies and private instrumentalities.

Assessing Institutional Development: The Legal Framework That Shapes Public Institutions

Thomas H. Stanton

Professional evaluators increasingly focus on the quality of institutions and how institutions affect economic and developmental outcomes (World Bank, Operations Evaluation Department, 1994). The quality of a country's institutions, in turn, is affected by the nature of its legal system (World Bank, 1994).

This chapter provides an introduction to the law of public institutions and how the law shapes institutions that provide goods and services to the public. (Institutions intended primarily to serve political, legislative, or judicial functions are not discussed.) This introduction is intended to help evaluators distinguish basic institutional types and understand how institutional choices can affect performance, capacity, accountability, and potential life cycles. Evaluators can then apply the conceptual framework of the law of public institutions to their diagnoses of the source of institutional shortcomings and the prescription of remedies.

The second section of this chapter outlines the legal framework that helps to determine the quality of public institutions. It distinguishes between (1) agencies of government, including departments and government enterprises, and (2) private instrumentalities of government, that is, private entities that serve public purposes under the law. The law governing each of these types of institution contrasts with the legal framework that applies to (3) private companies that serve private goals.

The chapter's third section reviews some of the ways in which the legal framework helps to determine the external environment, capacity and incentives, nature of service to public purposes, and life cycle of each type of institution. The

NEW DIRECTIONS FOR EVALUATION, no. 67, Fall 1995 © Jossey-Bass Publishers

concluding section suggests aspects of the legal framework of an institution that deserve scrutiny in an assessment of its quality.

This chapter represents the first part of a work in progress. It relies heavily on the author's analysis of the legal framework that shapes institutions in the United States (for example, Stanton, 1994a, 1994b) and on published studies of legal systems in other countries (for example, de Soto, 1989). The author welcomes feedback on the applicability of the concepts outlined in this chapter to particular institutions in developing countries.

Nature of Institutions

North (1990) and the new institutional economists have established that institutions matter and can help to determine a country's economic performance. The new institutional economics is producing a stream of important work concerning the economic rules of the game and how the qualities of a legal system can contribute to efficient markets (Williamson, 1994; Levy and Spiller, 1993). Those qualities include (1) clear rules that establish private rights, especially in property, (2) enforceable rules that parties can rely on in their transactions and contractual relationships, and (3) rules that represent a credible commitment to avoid arbitrary changes, for example in government economic regulation.

From a legal perspective, institutions are more than merely the economic rules of the game. They are the way a society chooses to organize itself to carry out public and private activities. Hurst reminds us that, besides the market, institutions of society may include the family, the church, publicly and privately organized education, science, and technology: "Wherever we encounter substantial, continued, organized activity with means structured to pursue shared goals, we deal with behavior that at some stage of consequence can be called institutional" (1977, p. 48).

Institutions are shaped by the law—the publicly enforceable rules of the game—and institutions that serve public purposes are based upon public law. The quality of a system of public law relates to many of the characteristics identified by the new institutional economics, including clarity, enforceability, and commitment. It is important to add the feature of legitimacy: to be effective, laws must be accepted as legitimate by those to whom they apply. Lessons from the colonial period (Furnivall, 1956) and from communist rule (Massell, 1968) indicate that even a legal system backed by an overwhelming monopoly of force needs legitimacy to succeed. Empirical research would be useful to establish the relative importance, in determining the quality of institutions and governance, of the legitimacy of particular legal rules and imperfectly associated variables such as "democracy" (for example, Clague, Keefer, Knack, and Olson, 1994).

Trebilcock (1994) nicely frames the question of whether law and the legal system help to determine underlying social and economic realities, or whether the law depends on and is molded by those realities. Shirley (1994) similarly asks: How much is law destiny? How much can we achieve by changing the law? What causes a particular legal framework and how is it enforced?

None of these questions may be answerable in the abstract. A country's economic development may prompt reform of archaic restrictions in the legal system; the emergence of better legal forms in turn can facilitate further economic growth. In many cases it may be just as important to get the institutions—including the legal framework—right as it is to get the economics right. A simple linear progression (Williamson, 1994) may not capture adequately the complexities of the underlying relationships of institutions, law, and economics.

Public Versus Private Institutions. A government makes a threshold decision when it selects an institution to serve public purposes. The basic choice of whether the institution is public or private affects the manner in which the intended public purposes will be served.

Government agencies include departments and bureaus that carry out governmental functions and public enterprises. With Gray (1984, p. 41), one can usefully define a public enterprise as one controlled by the government, producing goods and services for sale as its primary function, and operating under a policy that its revenues should cover at least a substantial part of its costs. In countries governed by a civil code system of law, the formal designation of an enterprise as public or private may vary for sometimes inconsistent reasons (Friedmann, 1954). (This chapter does not discuss agencies of sublevels of government such as localities.)

Private instrumentalities of government are privately owned and managed. Like government institutions, and unlike ordinary private firms, private government instrumentalities are permitted to engage only in those activities that are authorized by their enabling legislation. Often these restrictions involve application of detailed prescriptions by a government regulator. Private instrumentalities include investor-owned firms, cooperative enterprises, and nonprofit organizations. This chapter discusses only investor-owned and profit-oriented instrumentalities, typical examples of which are investor-owned utilities such as railroads, power companies, or telecommunications firms, and banks and other financial institutions.

Private institutions may potentially offer better capability than that available from the state. In the age of mercantilism, private instrumentalities of government provided a broad range of services including mining, banking, and trade at a time when governments lacked the capability to provide such services through public agencies. Privatized firms often become instrumentalities of government if they provide services that by law are considered to embody a public purpose, for example as regulated monopolies. (Aharoni, 1986, traces the historical relationship of public enterprises and private instrumentalities in various countries.)

The different laws applicable to public and private institutions shape them differently. Table 3.1 shows some of the ways in which laws may differ in their application to private instrumentalities of government and government agencies.

Table 3.1. Legal Characteristics of Ordinary Companies Versus Private Instrumentalities Versus Government Agencies

Ordinary Companies	Private Instrumentalities	Government Agencies
Organized under generally applicable laws to serve private purposes	Organized to serve public purposes; are considered instrumentalities of government	Organized as part of the government to serve public purposes
Can usually obtain a license to do business by registering with a government department	Must obtain a charter from (1) the legislature or (2) an administrative agency according to statutory standards	Created by specific authority of law
Authorized to conduct all activities except as expressly prohibited by law	Authorized to conduct only those activities expressly permitted by their charters	Authorized to conduct only those activities expressly permitted by law
Can freely enter lines of business except where entry is prohibited by law; can freely stop serving markets or customers	Can only enter lines of business expressly authorized by law; may be required to serve particular markets or customers	Can only provide services expressly authorized by law; may be required to provide particular types of service
Generally have no unique benefits granted by law; often operate in contested markets	Have unique benefits granted by law to a single company or category of companies; often protected by law from entry by competitors	Have special benefits granted by law and sovereign privileges and immunities unless expressly waived by law; often monopolist in the provision of public goods and services
Often unregulated	Usually regulated	Regulated by other agencies, for example, with respect to budget
Can be forced into bankruptcy by unsatisfied customers	Probably cannot be forced into bankruptcy, even if insolvent; must be terminated by government action	Generally have sovereign immunity from bankruptcy; must be terminated by law

The legal framework of ordinary private companies is presented as a benchmark to illustrate the distinctive characteristics of the three basic forms of institution.

Combining Governmental and Private Attributes. Governments often have trouble combining the perceived strengths of public and private agencies into a single institution and should be cautious about the legal framework that they apply to such hybrids (Seidman, 1988). The public enterprise is a case in point. Ideally, the public enterprise is expected to be controlled by government but to operate in accordance with commercial principles to provide goods and services on a potentially self-sustaining basis. The availability of a revenue stream to support operations means that a public enterprise might be held accountable through its economic performance rather than through many of the input and procedural controls (especially the budget) that usually apply to government agencies (Seidman, 1983). Also, at least in theory, the public enterprise may be able to allocate resources more efficiently than a private company that is driven by the need to increase profits and returns for private investors.

In practice, governments often use their enterprises to serve a wide range of noneconomic as well as economic purposes (Gray, 1984). Public enterprises in many developing countries, for example, may provide goods and services on such highly preferential terms that they come to be "increasingly illiquid or on the verge of financial collapse" (Shirley and Nellis, 1991, p. 63). The net result can be a public enterprise that is not sufficiently accountable either to the government or to the marketplace and whose performance manifests both inefficiencies and allocative inequities (Floyd, 1984).

Pitfalls may occur when a government uses private instrumentalities for public purposes. To serve noneconomic ends, governments may hold the prices of private instrumentalities at unprofitable levels, require service to uneconomic market segments, or fail to adjust the legal powers of instrumentalities in time to meet emerging forms of competition. In such cases, they risk driving an instrumentality into financial failure. However, because the instrumentality is privately owned and managed, its failure may precipitate much greater financial loss than if it were either a government agency or a completely private company. This is especially true when a government tries to provide a financial guarantee for the obligations of a private instrumentality. (Stanton, 1994a, explores these issues for financial institutions, such as banks, that are instrumentalities of government.)

Institutional Consequences of the Legal Framework

Differences in the legal framework cause fundamental differences in the performance, accountability, capacity, and life cycle of public versus private institutions. See Table 3.2, in which, again, ordinary private companies are presented as a benchmark.

Government Agencies. Government agencies are owned by the government and controlled by government officials. Created by law, they depend upon the terms of law to determine their capacity, accountability,

Table 3.2. Institutional Consequences of the Legal Characteristics of Ordinary Companies Versus Private Instrumentalities Versus Government Agencies

Ordinary Companies	Private Instrumentalities	Government Agencies
External environment is more market-based than political	External environment includes the market, but political factors tend to dominate	Political factors predominate; the market affects some public enterprises
Accountable to private owners	Accountable to private owners; often regulated by government as well	Accountable to multiple parts of government and to influential constituencies
Financial disclosure to private owners; if a publicly held firm, also required public disclosures	Financial disclosure to private owners and possibly to government regulators	Some public disclosure; often less financial disclosure than is required for private firms
Market-based external controls based on financial performance	Market-based external controls plus regulatory controls	Often heavy controls on inputs (for example, budget and staffing) and procedures; public enterprises may have greater autonomy
Profit-orientated goals often force focus on particular activities, market segments, and strategies	Mix of profit-oriented goals and regulated service; orientation to serving diffuse purposes	Diffuse political pressures lead to serving multiple purposes that often may not be articulated
Life cycle: thrives or goes out of business. Forced exit of failed firms	Often stagnate over time; government backing can forestall easy exit until institution fails at great cost	Tend to stagnate over time, without ceasing to exist; for example, primary function may shift from providing services to providing employment

and activities. Their staff are appointed according to law to offices or positions authorized by law. They are often subject to controls that tend to prescribe procedures and inputs rather than performance and outputs. They are funded through a budget process authorized by law.

As institutions that serve public purposes, government agencies have strengths and limitations. The strengths involve the direct accountability of government agencies to policy makers, responsiveness to changing public priorities, and ability to serve constituencies whose financial standing might be considered marginal. The limitations relate to the conspicuous lack of operational capacity at some agencies, often including limited resources for staffing and systems. The combination of inadequate resources and managerial inflexibility means that the government may lack the capacity to administer some programs, either directly through government agencies or indirectly through regulated private instrumentalities, without risking significant financial losses.

Private Instrumentalities. As private sector institutions, private instrumentalities may be subject to performance controls in the form of the financial bottom line. The advantages of using private sector institutions relate to their ability to use resources efficiently in search of profits. When necessary to achieve profitability, private firms will tend to invest in high quality personnel and systems that can be far more productive than those found in government. A disadvantage of using profit-seeking companies is that they are likely to place the financial interests of private owners above the government's interests in promoting service for public purposes. This disadvantage can be compounded in countries that have private monopolies (for example as a result of having privatized state enterprises) but lack an effective legal framework to deal with the consequences—for allocative efficiency and the distribution of benefits—of the activities of such companies.

In return for the limitations imposed by law, private instrumentalities receive benefits such as tax privileges, subsidized loans, special access to foreign exchange, and government guarantees of their obligations, and sometimes protection from the entry of potential competitors into the market. Such governmental benefits loosen the competitive discipline that can help keep firms lean and efficient.

On the other hand, an instrumentality can suffer from impaired capacity if the law confines it to an inadequate market segment. Although the government may assure a profitable and protected market niche at the start of an instrumentality's life, changes in technologies and competition can erode the advantages of the legally protected market. Public utilities, railroads, or financial institutions, for example, may find that evolving markets reduce the value of their current franchise, threatening their ability to thrive.

Politics Versus Market Discipline. Table 3.2 illustrates how the single most important aspect of the legal framework relates to whether an institution is public or private. If an institution is a government agency, then political factors predominate in its external environment. The agency is accountable to multiple parts of the government and to various influential constituencies. This usually results in the imposition of diffuse, even inconsistent, and poorly articulated goals. A special category of government agency is the public enterprise, which is accountable to political factors and constituencies but also possibly to market forces.

Ordinary private companies are affected by an entirely different set of laws, which ideally will create an external environment determined much more by the market than by politics. The profit motive results in much more operational focus than may be possible for a government agency, but the company has no legal responsibility to serve those customers or market segments that it finds unprofitable.

Somewhere in between are the various private instrumentalities of government, including banks and other financial institutions, regulated monopolies such as utilities, and other firms whose activities are considered to embody a public purpose under the law. As privately owned firms, these institutions tend to serve the most profitable parts of their legally permitted markets. This contrasts to the government institution that is more motivated within the limits of its budget to serve all people who are eligible recipients of its services.

Instrumentalities are accountable also to the government, including the lawmakers who can expand, contract, or otherwise change their legal mandates and benefits, and any relevant government regulators. Thus, although the market is an important part of the external environment, political factors often dominate. Although the goals of instrumentalities relate to the conditions in the market, government may impose diffuse purposes at variance with pure profitability, such as requirements to serve noneconomic market segments.

Once instrumentalities have become profitable, the government can find it difficult to influence their activities, either with respect to serving new and evolving public priorities or with respect to reducing financial exposure from their activities. Because private instrumentalities can live or die according to the terms of their enabling legislation, they have an incentive to use resources to dominate the legislature, their designated regulators, and others in government who might threaten their legal franchise or otherwise impose policies at variance with the interests of the private owners.

The Problem of Exit. Ideally, the private firm that fails financially can be thrown into bankruptcy under a well-defined bankruptcy law and its resources reallocated to more productive uses. Government agencies and programs do not automatically exit when they fail to serve a useful purpose; it is hard for a government to terminate a governmental activity.

Some government agencies, when backed by powerful constituencies, may continue to draw resources long after their nominal public purposes have declined in public priority. Indeed, a government subsidy can increase the number and strength of constituents of a program, thereby increasing the strength of an "iron rice bowl" that can become very costly. This pattern has been observed especially with respect to public enterprises, both in the developing world and in economically more developed countries.

Similar problems of exit may exist for private instrumentalities of government. The law may prevent instrumentalities from becoming bankrupt like private firms. Instead, it may provide that instrumentalities can be reorganized or wound up only by action of the government, possibly through a designated regulator of a particular instrumentality. For instrumentalities receiving certain kinds of subsidies, this distinction can be of fundamental importance: because of their access to special subsidies, private instrumentalities may be able to continue their activities long after they have failed financially.

Conclusions

Institutional Quality and the Legal Framework. The problems of government agencies are likely to be those of confusion about mission, inadequate capacity, and failure to be held accountable for the achievement of performance goals. By contrast, problems of private (investor-owned) instrumentalities that serve public purposes are likely to be those of missions that emphasize efficiency goals but neglect distributional goals, government's lack of capacity to hold these institutions accountable, and vulnerability to a mix of private ownership and governmental benefits that raises the likelihood of expensive failures.

Government agencies are more likely to stagnate than to die. A private instrumentality may begin by reaping handsome profits within its legally prescribed market segment but become vulnerable to new forms of competition or to escalating legal or regulatory requirements to serve unprofitable market segments.

More generally, if laws are the enforceable rules of the game, then it is important to understand the elements of institutional quality that are reflected in the legal system of a particular country. The new institutional economics has begun this effort with respect to laws applicable to ordinary private firms. Many economists would like to see the legal system provide a framework that promotes efficient behavior among parties, for example with respect to property rights, enforceability of contracts, and government commitment to avoid arbitrary changes in economic regulation.

The historical lessons of law and development add the important criterion of legitimacy. Ideally, law should reflect the values of a society, including its cultural, social, and distributional concerns. The expressions of social values in law are especially important when they apply to government agencies, including public enterprises, and private instrumentalities. Here, the whole point of many legal requirements may be to assure that public institutions serve noneconomic values. The World Bank's increasing emphasis on governance (World Bank, 1994) is a valuable step in assessing the nature of the tradeoff between economic and noneconomic values that are reflected in the legal framework of private and public institutions.

Assessing Institutional Quality. The professional evaluator, mesmerized neither by the concepts of law nor those of economics, can play a valuable role. In the application of the framework of this chapter to assessing institutional quality, the threshold issues involve the assessment of the respective roles of politics versus the market. A diagnosis might proceed as follows:

Is a particular public or private institution subject to market discipline? If so, could the legal framework be enhanced to promote the application of market discipline—for example, by improving public disclosure requirements for investors, or by improving the effectiveness of bankruptcy procedures?

If an institution is a private instrumentality, to what extent is it subject to market discipline? Could this discipline be enhanced through market-based improvements such as more efficient exit procedures or the removal of laws that may impose barriers to entry by competitors? Could some subsidies be phased out to increase the competitive pressure on the instrumentality to be efficient? Could cross subsidies and their consequences be made more transparent and more clearly understood in the political process? Could the form of subsidies be changed so that the instrumentality can serve designated unprofitable market segments in the most efficient manner? Could explicit or implicit government guarantees be removed, so that increased market discipline can encourage practices that reduce the cost of failure of firms that otherwise would not exit in time?

If the institution is a government agency that provides goods and services, could alternative institutional forms provide such goods and services more efficiently while respecting the noneconomic values that may also apply? Here, the framework of Kessides (1993) is an excellent model of institutional options that deserves to be applied to a broad range of economic activities of government. An important underlying issue relates to the capacity of a government agency, either to deliver goods and services directly or to supervise competently the private parties it employs to deliver those goods and services.

Professional evaluators of institutions in developing countries are ideally positioned to enhance the body of knowledge about the law of public institutions that can be applied across a broad range of countries, legal systems, and intended public purposes.

References

Aharoni, Y. *The Evolution and Management of State-Owned Enterprises.* Cambridge, Mass.: Ballinger Publishing Company, 1986.

Clague, C., Keefer, P., Knack, S., and Olson, M. "Institutions and Economic Performance: A New Look at Democracies and Growth." Draft prepared for the Institutional Reform and the Informal Sector Conference on Economic and Political Institutions for Sustainable Development, 1994.

de Soto, H. *The Other Path: The Invisible Revolution in the Third World.* New York: Harper-Collins, 1989.

Floyd, R. H. "Some Topical Issues Concerning Public Enterprises." In R. H. Floyd, C. S. Gray, and R. P. Short (eds.), *Public Enterprise in Mixed Economies: Some Macroeconomic Aspects.* Washington, D.C.: International Monetary Fund, 1984, 1–34.

Friedmann, W. "A Comparative Analysis." In W. Friedmann (ed.), *The Public Corporation: A Comparative Symposium.* Toronto: Carswell Company, 1954.

Furnivall, J. S. *Colonial Policy and Practice.* New York: New York University Press, 1956.

Gray, C. S. "Toward a Conceptual Framework for Macroeconomic Evaluation of Public Enterprise Performance in Mixed Economies." In R. H. Floyd, C. S. Gray, and R. P. Short (eds.), *Public Enterprise in Mixed Economies: Some Macroeconomic Aspects.* Washington, D.C.: International Monetary Fund, 1984, 35–109.

Hurst, J. W. *Law and Social Order in the United States.* Ithaca, N.Y.: Cornell University Press, 1977.

Kessides, C. *Institutional Options for the Provision of Infrastructure.* World Bank Discussion Paper. Washington, D.C.: World Bank, 1993.

Levy, B., and Spiller, P. T. "Regulation, Institutions, and Commitment in Telecommunications: A Comparative Analysis of Five Country Studies." Paper presented at the Annual Bank Conference on Development Economics. Washington, D.C.: World Bank, 1993.

Massell, G. J. "Law as an Instrument of Revolutionary Change in a Traditional Milieu: The Case of Soviet Central Asia." *Law and Society Review,* 1968, 2, 179–228.

North, D. C. *Institutions, Institutional Change, and Economic Performance.* Cambridge, Mass.: Cambridge University Press, 1990.

Seidman, H. "Public Enterprise Autonomy: Need for a New Theory." *International Review of Administrative Sciences,* 1983, Mar., 3–18.

Seidman, H. "The Quasi-World of the Federal Government." *Brookings Review,* 1988, Summer, 23–27.

Shirley, M. Discussion of paper on "Assessing Institutional Development." Remarks delivered at the World Bank Conference on Evaluation and Development, Washington, D.C., Dec., 1994.

Shirley, M., and Nellis, J. *Public Enterprise Reform: The Lessons of Experience.* Economic Development Institute of the World Bank. Washington, D.C.: World Bank, 1991.

Stanton, T. H. "Federal Credit Programs: The Economic Consequences of Institutional Choices." *The Financier: Analyses of Capital and Money Market Transactions,* 1994a, Feb., 20–34.

Stanton, T. H. "Nonquantifiable Risks and Financial Institutions: The Mercantilist Legal Framework of Banks, Thrifts, and·Government-Sponsored Enterprises." In C. A. Stone and A. Zissu (eds.), *Global Risk-Based Capital Regulations,* Vol.1. Homewood, Ill.: Irwin Professional Publishing, 1994b, 57–97.

Trebilcock, M. J. "The Institutional Preconditions to Economic Development: What Do We Know?" Unpublished manuscript, Oct. 25, 1994.

Williamson, O. E. "Institutions and Economic Organization: The Governance Perspective." Paper presented at Annual Bank Conference on Development Economics. Washington, D.C.: World Bank, 1994.

World Bank. *Governance: The World Bank's Experience.* Washington, D.C.: World Bank, 1994.

World Bank, Operations Evaluation Department. "Institutional Development." *1992 Evaluation Results.* Washington, D.C.: World Bank, 1994, 123–155.

THOMAS H. STANTON is a Washington, D.C., attorney and a fellow of the Center for the Study of American Government at the Johns Hopkins University, where he teaches the law of public institutions.

PART TWO

Impacts and Instruments

Why do so many environmental projects develop unforeseen problems?
The survival of flawed projects is due to biases in their selection and
appraisal, compounded by weaknesses in evaluation methods and
inadequate organizational learning processes.

Evaluating Environmental Impacts: The Process of Unnatural Selection

James T. Winpenny

This chapter describes how the environmental impacts of projects are currently evaluated, analyzes why current procedures are unsatisfactory, and considers what can be done, with some implications for development practitioners. The focus is on projects, or programs in the sense of clusters of projects, rather than on policies, even though policies may be amenable to the same kinds of analysis and evaluation as are considered here. "Environmental" projects (hereafter EPs for brevity) will mean any discrete activities likely to have a substantial impact on the environment, either positive or negative. For the purpose of project evaluation it is important to distinguish between projects that explicitly seek to benefit the environment and those with other purposes that have environmental side effects. Many of the criticisms aired in this chapter are of the latter kind of project.

In fact, many points made here could apply to any type of project, in any sector, but are believed to apply with greater force to EPs. The latter are characterized by effects that may not have been anticipated, often take a long time to emerge, and are difficult to detect. Some environmental effects also are irreversible. EPs typically involve institutional issues and reforms, which are a further source of problems. These and other features render EPs especially prone to the biases and risks discussed below.

Current Practice

For environmental as for other projects, the main approaches to performance evaluation are ex post economic appraisal, subjective scoring methods, and impact evaluation. Most leading development agencies combine more than one of these, using both quantitative and qualitative criteria for analysis. Traditionally, evaluation has been biased towards the use of economic reappraisals, though these were unsuitable for certain kinds of projects. In the last two decades economic approaches have been complemented by the use of other methods, recognizing the greater complexity of projects' aims and effects.

Ex post economic appraisal assesses the effectiveness of a project in relation to its original goals by substituting actual outturn data for the assumptions made at the time of appraisal. The overall method and choice of variables is kept constant to enable a valid comparison to be made. This approach depends on the validity of the original appraisal. If the original appraisal was flawed, biased, or too narrow, or if criteria have changed in the meantime, the evaluation's conclusions will be impaired. Enough time must be allowed for trends in benefits and recurrent costs to assert themselves.

Subjective scoring rates effectiveness by inviting an "expert" jury to score and rank different projects on the basis of stated criteria. This is sometimes known as the Delphi Technique. On the one hand, it is a way of allowing wider, nonquantifiable, and more subjective criteria—which, in their place, are perfectly valid—to enter into the judgment of effectiveness. On the other hand, subjective scoring exercises need to be well controlled if they are not to become arbitrary. If, for instance, a number of criteria are to be used, some quantifiable, others not, it is reasonable to canvass various different opinions on how the project has performed on the nonquantifiable criteria, but the relative weights of the different criteria must be agreed on from the outset.

Impact evaluation arose out of a suspicion that reworking economic cost/benefit analyses might omit important effects of a project and would say little about how far the project's original aims were fulfilled. As described by Berlage and Stokke (1992), impact analysis assesses the effects of an intervention on its surroundings. The assessment may cover a multiplicity of aspects, including technical, economic, sociocultural, institutional, and environmental changes.

The rise of impact evaluation reflects concerns in particular about the distributional impact of aid projects on target groups, especially the poor, women, children, and the landless. Concerns about the environment have reinforced the desire to trace a project's impact on its physical as well as social surroundings. For instance, the evaluation of water supply projects would be incomplete without assessing their impact on the amount of water used, its quality, its impact on women, health, community involvement, and so forth (Rahman and McDonnell, 1985).

Multicriteria analysis of project performance normally includes the quantifiable economic rate of return, where available, and—depending on the type of project and their relevance—other criteria such as cost per beneficiary, range and scope (number of beneficiaries), distribution of benefits, ease and speed of implementation, and replicability.

Just as projects themselves have become more complex and multifaceted over time as their goals have multiplied, so too have evaluation methods. Most economic evaluations of projects incorporate a comparison of outturn results with appraisal forecasts, but it is more common now to supplement the quantified economic evaluations with judgments based on a range of other criteria. Some of these are quantified but not in monetary form; others are nonquantifiable and involve a greater degree of judgment.

Why Current Procedures Are Flawed

Experience points to the conclusion that environmental projects are subject to bias in the way they are chosen and appraised and in the way they are subsequently evaluated. These biases compound each other to produce a portfolio of environmentally unfriendly development schemes. Over time, the biases result in a Darwinian unnatural selection: projects are conceived in environmental innocence and handicapped in their ability to deal with their environmental impacts when these inevitably surface.

The causes of this problem can be discussed under the headings of appraisal optimism, environmental astigmatism, methodological weaknesses, and evaluation biases.

Appraisal Optimism. A pervasive syndrome in development agencies is appraisal optimism. Rates of return tend to be lower at project completion than those estimated at the time of appraisal and to fall further over time. Where outcomes are uncertain, appraisers tend to assume the best, perhaps influenced by the need to show a minimum rate of return to get the project accepted and by the imperative to disburse (Little and Mirrlees, 1991; Lipton and Toye, 1990). This implies that projects are selected that are systematically weaker than they appear, and that insufficient attention is paid to features that turn out to be sources of weakness. By the same token, measures that might reduce these downside risks are not properly considered.

Following an exhaustive internal review of World Bank staff appraisal reports, a study carried out for the World Bank (World Bank, 1992) lent authority to the above conclusions. Because the risks of projects are not properly taken into account, appraisal rates of return contain a systematic upward bias, and this bias has increased. It is therefore almost inevitable that *ex post* rates of return should be lower, in many cases unacceptably so—a fact crushingly demonstrated by Pohl and Mihaljek (1992) in an analysis of more than 1,000 World Bank projects.

At this point in the argument we should note that EPs are not necessarily more prone than others to appraisal optimism, which is a widespread syndrome. But we now turn to other factors that we would expect to apply disproportionately to EPs.

Environmental Astigmatism. The normal "appraisal optimism" that leads to the selection of flawed projects is aggravated by a blindness to environmental risks, which if properly anticipated and quantified would reduce expected rates of return even further. Evidence increasingly indicates that a failure to discern potential environmental effects is harmful to project performance. This point obviously only applies to EPs whose environmental impacts are an incidental byproduct. Preliminary evidence is that a cohort of EPs with explicit environmental objectives, often embodying physical "environment friendly" components, have performed better than projects aimed at poverty reduction (World Bank, 1995).

A subset of World Bank projects with actual or presumed environmental impacts was evaluated and showed a disproportionate tendency for projects to have disappointing or unacceptable rates of return (Ascher, 1992). Many reasons were adduced for this outcome: unexpected negative feedback through effects on ecosystems (for example through build-up of resistance to pesticide, contamination of water in aquaculture fisheries, or spread of waterborne disease); delays pending environmental mitigation measures; delays due to opposition from political or environmental parties; and other unexpected physical reactions (such as siltation of reservoirs and channels, salinization, or soil erosion).

On a positive note, evidence suggests that an increasing number of development projects are subject to some kind of environmental assessment (EA), which is a precondition of more accurate analysis and more informed decisions. The latest review of the use of EA in the World Bank found that more than half of all projects at the pre-approval stage were subject to some degree of EA, and that one fourth (by value—those in the Bank's "Category A") were given full EA. Nevertheless, the review uncovered problems with the process of EA: very limited consultation with affected populations and nongovernmental organizations, limited use of EA in project design (as opposed to a reactive "add-on"), and weak analysis of alternatives, mitigation measures, monitoring, and institutional aspects (World Bank, 1994).

The use of EA by other donors is of recent origin: evaluations done of German (Borries and others, 1990) and Danish (Danish International Development Agency, 1987) aid show that environmental issues were neglected or marginalized, even in dam schemes.

Methodological Weaknesses. Even if a project's environmental effects are understood, the methodology of appraisal often minimizes their impact on the economic internal rate of return (EIRR). It is now widely accepted that environmental effects tend to be overlooked or undervalued in economic analysis, and much guidance is now available on how this situation can be remedied (for example Dixon, Scura, Carpenter, and Sherman, 1994). The most common omission is the proper valuation of a project's externalities—its effects on parties other than those making the decisions.

The author recently undertook an (unpublished) review of thirty projects of a major multilateral agency. For the sample reviewed, quantification of environmental costs and benefits would have improved EIRRs in urban water, natural gas-based energy, social forestry, and watershed management and flood control projects. It would have lowered EIRRs in irrigation, thermal power, heavy industry, agricultural processing, land settlement, aquaculture, low-income housing, and new town development. In a few cases, the results could be attributed to project-specific factors (design, location), but in most cases the results were predictable because of systematic biases in the way the environmental costs and benefits were reckoned.

The same exercise revealed that urban water supply schemes suffer invidious comparisons with those in other sectors because of the methodology used to calculate benefits, which uses financial internal rates of returns (FIRRs) as minimum estimates of EIRRs. Such rates of return are not comparable with those estimated for projects in other sectors of the economy. The fuller use of "willingness to pay" (WTP) estimates of benefits in the appraisal of urban water projects would tend to improve these projects' EIRRs and, other things equal, increase the number of such projects in the agency's portfolio. Similarly, if it were possible to quantify the benefits of improved sewerage, at present a very elusive task, this would help to overcome some of the resistance among borrowing governments to what are perceived as "social" and "nonproductive" projects.

Some urban water schemes were approved without taking into account the cost of watershed conservation. This is true more generally of irrigation projects, which tended to be approved without taking account of the costs of upland protection works, and which postponed essential drainage work until project implementation was well underway. Internalizing both types of cost as part of the initial appraisal would probably have led to fewer irrigation projects being approved.

Taking systematic account of the environmental costs and benefits of projects can and should change the way projects are conceived and designed. In many cases, the change in design will result from the attempt to internalize external environmental costs, for example by having polluters pay for pollution abatement. Such changes also may result from causes other than the need to quantify environmental effects; they may be needed, for example, to conform to local legislation or to conform to "best practice" guidelines. Quantifying their effects can sharpen the argument by indicating the magnitudes involved, and the size of the tradeoff between economic and environmental aims where these conflict.

If previously unquantified effects are routinely valued and weighed in the overall EIRR, one can expect these aspects of the project to receive more attention in future. For example, several regional development programs looked distinctly marginal based on their agricultural development components, but a number of environmental benefits stemming from the components had been excluded from the calculation. If these benefits could have been valued and weighed in the appraisal, more attention probably would have been paid to these components, and more money spent on them.

One aspect of project design is the accompanying package of conditions. Certain projects can be shown to have potential environmental effects but to require adjustments in policy to mitigate costs or realize benefits. A road improvement project indirectly caused environmental problems through land speculation and development blight. Stricter land use planning and conservation measures would have helped to mitigate these effects.

The improved valuation of environmental effects clarifies the size of gains and losses from a project and who bears them. This provides information useful for cost recovery or redistributional purposes. It can provide data for setting prices, taxes, subsidies, and compensation payments. Better assessment of the size of project benefits can help pricing. A series of studies of urban water consumption in recent years has uncovered a considerable and previously unsuspected willingness to pay for improved supplies, even among the poorest groups of society (Whittington, Lauria, and Mu, 1991). This is often sufficient to justify piped supplies, charged at an economic rate.

Applying the principle of "polluter pays," or its cynical relative "victim pays," requires some estimation of the costs involved, which valuation can provide. Watershed conservation projects benefit downstream users such as irrigated farmers, hydropower utilities, and municipal water supply operators. In some cases the "victims" have started paying to preserve their watershed. In one case, a power utility has taken over responsibility for managing the watershed over its reservoir in order to arrest siltation (Southgate and Macke, 1989).

Another source of methodological bias is the omission of any depletion premium or user cost in estimating the costs of extracting natural capital. When oil, gold, or groundwater is extracted, part of its cost of production is the opportunity cost of the reduced availability of that good in future. One measure is the extra cost that society incurs in future to produce substitutes for these resources, as when new water supplies are developed to replace diminished groundwater stocks (Munasinghe, 1990).

A recent survey of twenty-three World Bank projects undertaken since the mid 1980s discovered that in most projects no costs were attributed to the depletion of natural capital. This applied to a range of sectors: minerals, natural gas and petroleum, forestry, fisheries, and livestock (Kellenberg and Daly, 1994, following the previous work of Amsberg, 1993).

The depletion principle applies not only to the obvious finite resources such as minerals and hydrocarbons but also to renewable resources exploited beyond their sustainable yield (for example, forests, fisheries, farmland, and pasture). It also applies—though here quantification is more difficult—to the life-support services of the atmosphere and biosphere and to natural waste assimilation functions, all of which may be stretched beyond their capacity. Omitting the opportunity cost of a resource that is being depleted means that the user cost of the resource is underestimated, encouraging the over-consumption of the resource.

Social cost/benefit analysis as used in international donor agencies has been criticized on the grounds that it has not been widely applied in practice and has distracted from more important determinants of project performance. Certainly many factors other than the analytical quality of a proposal weigh in the decision to proceed with a project, and it would be naive to overlook "public choice" factors in investment decisions (Tullock, 1987). However, this is no reason not to seek the best possible appraisal.

More weighty is the argument that more attention should be paid to the impact of policies and institutions on project performance, the use of realistic assumptions about institutional capacity and relevant macroeconomic framework, and the rigorous use of risk and sensitivity analysis in project design (World Bank, 1992).

Evaluation Biases. Much of our knowledge about the performance of projects derives from *ex post* evaluation studies carried out quite soon after the projects are formally completed. These reports note how economic returns have been affected by unanticipated changes in the costs, implementation periods, or prices of inputs and outputs assumed at appraisal. But they are often carried out too soon to detect the longer-term performance of a project, let alone its contribution to "sustainable development" (Ascher, 1992).

The essence of environmental effects is that they often take many years to emerge and sometimes take a complicated course. Relatively few evaluation studies track the long-term performance of projects with an environmental dimension. One of the lessons of the evaluation literature is that the longer-term performance of projects is not easy to predict at appraisal or even soon after formal completion. Many environmental disasters may not show up at evaluation. In this sense, "evaluation optimism" may be present as well; disturbing evidence suggests that most evaluations carried out a number of years after completion show even lower returns than those done at completion.

However, the notion of evaluation optimism may be taken too far. Just as newspapers focus on bad news, most evaluations focus on negative factors, examining project shortfalls from the viewpoint of agency targets and procedures. There is a danger of missing the growth of the forest by looking too closely at some stunted trees. Thus, a recent evaluation of World Bank EPs in Brazil drew attention to the need to take into account induced development impacts and interregional linkages (Redwood, 1993).

One of the earliest and best evaluation studies of development projects—a group of World Bank projects that were started in the 1950s—asserted the principle of the Hiding Hand (Hirschman, 1967). The argument is that providence conceals future disappointments and aggravation from the current generation of project appraisers and managers; if they only knew, they would hesitate to proceed. Project sponsors are optimistic about things going wrong with their projects, pessimistic about their ability to deal with them, and wrong on both counts.

This should not be interpreted to mean that ignorance is bliss, or that the less known about the project the better (Picciotto, 1994). The moral is rather that project sponsors should not expect their projects to go smoothly but should try to anticipate what might go wrong and develop the knowledge and skills to cope.

The current evaluation literature is catching up with what Hirschman wrote thirty years ago. A gathering consensus maintains that project sustainability depends on "capacity building" and fostering "problem solving" ability, qualities that are tested by and may thrive on the kind of reverses that are the stuff of the evaluation literature.

One of the fundamental differences between "good" and "bad" projects is the ability of the projects' sponsors and management to solve the problems thrown up during implementation. Problem solving and learning by doing are crucial aspects of capacity building, as noted by Lipton and Toye (1990) for India. It is difficult for ex ante appraisal to anticipate these factors. One review of large USAID projects argued that the design and implementation of projects are more akin to art than science, and that they rely on commitment, flexibility, innovation, and a belief in human progress (Gow and Morss, 1988).

What Is to Be Done?

Several of the criticisms aired above apply to projects of all descriptions. They have received added force from the growth of environmental concerns. Addressing them calls for action on a number of fronts.

Information Gathering. Our understanding of environmental processes is poor, and our assessment of the environmental implications of human activity is blinkered. The need for thorough, widely focused, and imaginative environmental assessment cannot be too highly stressed. Experience in implementing the project is the best kind of data generation—a point reverted to below in considering project design. Meanwhile, the ground for a project should be thoroughly prepared with baseline surveys, environmental assessments, and systems to monitor key environmental indicators.

Revising Appraisal Methods. This chapter has dwelt heavily on the shortcomings of conventional appraisal methods because much evaluation is based on the reworking of original appraisals, using the old methodology. If we are looking ahead to a new age of more enlightened evaluation, we must start by reforming appraisal methods. Better appraisal is a necessary, if not a sufficient, condition for better projects, and this alone would be sufficient justification for the emphasis we place on it.

Appraisal of environmental projects should be improved by:

More economic valuation of environmental costs and benefits
Inclusion of depletion premia in projects entailing the use of natural resources
Fuller treatment of risk and uncertainty
Anticipation of events that might seriously affect the project's performance in future, including policy changes and other exogenous factors, and modelling the impact of these changes on the project through sensitivity and switching analysis
Identification of benefit and performance indicators to be monitored

"Model" appraisals and evaluations along these lines, combining environmental assessment and valuation, are urgently needed.

Revising Evaluation Criteria and Procedures. Much evaluation is based on results at or soon after project completion. More evaluation studies are required of projects with a number of years' operating experience. Many evaluations are too narrowly focused and risk missing crucial aspects of project effectiveness. The overwhelming bulk of evaluation studies concentrates on negative factors, explaining shortfalls in project performance that can be minimized through reforms in agencies' procedures. Hirschman's insights about the enduring value of problem solving have been lost on all but a few subsequent evaluators (Picciotto, 1994). More evaluations need to be done of successful projects, including the identification of "success" traits. This would entail taking a broader and longer view than is now customary and paying more attention to changes made to the project at the design stage, during implementation, and in the operating mode.

Redesigning Projects. Many projects are designed in ignorance of their potential environmental impacts. Project design should improve as a result of the more systematic assembly of environmental data through EA, research and evaluation, and the application of better appraisal methods. However, interest in more radical reforms to project design are increasing, spurred by what many people see as the special characteristics of environmental projects. Their argument is that environmental processes, and the impact of human interventions on them, are largely shrouded in mystery and take a long time to reveal themselves. When they do, the processes may be irreversible and even catastrophic. In these circumstances, conventional approaches to the project cycle are insufficient. Feasibility studies, baseline surveys, and risk and sensitivity analysis, desirable though they are, are not enough.

It is argued that a new project model is required, summarized in the slogans "listening, piloting, demonstrating, and mainstreaming" (LPDM). Listening is code for the participation by the main stakeholders in planning, with the aim of building consensus for the project. Piloting would involve the implementation on a small scale of the project or parts of it in the hope that lessons could be learned for subsequent modification/replication, and that mistakes would be too small to be disastrous. Demonstration would build on the results of piloting to broaden support for the concept and would include training for key users and managers. Mainstreaming consists of launching a successfully tried and demonstrated concept as a fully fledged project or program worthy of replication (Picciotto and Weaving, 1994).

LPDM is thoroughly Hirschmanesque in its stress on generating information during implementation, building a consensus (or coalition) for change among the stakeholders, and creating problem solving and institutional capacity. All the evidence of the recent evaluation literature is that these features are vital to achieve sustainability. The approach is also justified by economic arguments for the value of information in situations of great uncertainty.

How far LPDM should be tried in individual cases will be influenced by such factors as practical feasibility, cost, and time. It is impossible to pilot a project that has a large critical minimum size, such as a major dam, steel works, or power station. The best that can be hoped for is a sufficiently long planning and consultation period and an adequate review of alternatives, followed by phased development with careful monitoring and feedback.

Another problem for LPDM is posed by environmental processes and effects that take a long time to emerge, such as groundwater contamination, the impact of deforestation on microclimates, the long-distance movement of silt from soil erosion, the impact of agroforestry on local ecology, the effect of air pollution on the mental development of children, and of course the long-term effects (or even the fact) of global warming. Research into all these issues is vitally important, but to envisage it occurring in an LPDM framework is unrealistic. Investments cannot wait that long.

However, that still leaves ample scope for LPDM. For such projects as soil conservation, anti-erosion measures, neighborhood improvement programs, small-scale irrigation schemes, new agronomic packages, and urban and village water supply schemes, the new approach would be perfectly feasible. It would help to overcome current resistance to change (and to cost recovery) from top-down planning and inappropriate project concepts. Because such programs tend to be nationwide, or at least widely replicable, it is important to get them right through such means as LPDM. Some of the effects, including externalities, of such projects should become evident within a three- to seven-year implementation period, which is soon enough to enable feedback into the main program.

References

Amsberg, J. von. *Project Evaluation and the Depletion of Natural Capital: An Application of the Sustainability Principle.* Environment Department Working Paper 56. Washington, D.C.: World Bank, 1993.

Ascher, W. *Coping with the Disappointing Rates of Return on Development Projects That Affect the Environment.* Development Economics Department Background Paper. Washington, D.C.: World Bank, 1992.

Berlage, L. and Stokke, O. (eds.). *Evaluating Development Assistance: Approaches and Methods.* London: Frank Cass, 1992.

Borries, J., and others. *Cross-Sectional Evaluation of 16 Dam Projects in Asia, Africa, Latin America, and Europe.* Bonn: German Federal Ministry for Economic Cooperation, 1990.

Danish International Development Agency (DANIDA). *Cross-Cutting Dimensions of DANIDA Evaluation Reports: Sustainability, Women and the Environment.* Copenhagen, 1987.

Dixon, J. A., Scura, L. F., Carpenter, R. A., and Sherman, P. B. *Economic Analysis of Environmental Impacts.* London: Earthscan, 1994.

Gow, D. D., and Morss, E. R. "The Notorious Nine: Critical Problems in Project Implementation." *World Development,* 1988, 16 (12).

Hirschman, A. O. *Development Projects Observed.* Washington D.C.: Brookings Institution, 1967.

Kellenberg, J., and Daly, H. *Counting User Cost in Evaluating Projects Involving Depletion of Natural Capital: World Bank Best Practice and Beyond.* Washington, D.C.: World Bank, 1994.

Lipton, M., and Toye, J. *Does Aid Work in India?* London and New York: Routledge, 1990.

Little, I.M.D., and Mirrlees, J. A. "Project Appraisal and Planning Twenty Years On." In *Proceedings of the World Bank Annual Conference on Development Economics, 1990.* Washington, D.C.: World Bank, 1991.

Munasinghe, M. *Managing Water Resources to Avoid Environmental Degradation: Policy Analysis and Application.* Environment Department Working Paper 41. Washington, D.C.: World Bank, 1990.

Picciotto, R. "Visibility and Disappointment: The New Role of Development Evaluation." In L. Rodwin and D. A. Schon (eds.), *Rethinking the Development Experience*. Washington, D.C.: Brookings Institution and the Lincoln Institute, 1994.

Picciotto, R., and Weaving, R. "A New Project Cycle for the World Bank?" *Finance & Development*, 1994, *31* (4).

Pohl, G., and Mihaljek, D. "Project Evaluation and Uncertainty in Practice: A Statistical Analysis of Rate-of-Return Divergences of 1,015 World Bank Projects." *World Bank Economic Review*, 1992, *6* (2).

Rahman, S., and McDonnell, N. "An Analysis of USAID Impact Evaluation Studies: Implications for the Future." *Scandinavian Journal of Development Alternatives*, 1985, *4* (3–4).

Redwood, J. *World Bank Approaches to the Environment in Brazil: A Review of Selected Projects*. World Bank Operations Evaluation Study. Washington, D.C.: World Bank, 1993.

Southgate, D., and Macke, R. "The Downstream Benefits of Soil Conservation in Third World Hydroelectric Watersheds." *Land Economics*, 1989, *65* (1).

Tullock, G. "Public Choice." In J. Eatwell and others (eds.), *New Palgrave Dictionary of Economics*. London: Macmillan, 1987.

Whittington, D., Lauria, D. T., and Mu, X. "A Study of Water Vending and Willingness to Pay for Water in Onitsha, Nigeria." *World Development*, 1991, *19* (2–3).

World Bank. *Effective Implementation: Key to Development Impact: Report of the Portfolio Management Task Force*. Washington, D.C.: World Bank, 1992.

World Bank. *Making Development Sustainable: The World Bank and the Environment, Fiscal 1994*. Washington, D.C.: World Bank, 1994.

World Bank, Operations Evaluation Department. *1993 Evaluation Results*. Washington, D.C.: World Bank, 1995.

JAMES T. WINPENNY *is a research fellow at the Overseas Development Institute, London.*

This chapter critically examines the appropriateness of a comprehensive performance measurement system, based on standard performance indicators, to agricultural and rural development programs in poor countries.

Measuring the Performance of Agricultural and Rural Development Programs

Krishna Kumar

By the mid 1980s, the major international donor agencies had reached broad consensus on the nature and focus of monitoring and evaluation in agricultural and rural development (ARD) projects. They had agreed that at the project level, monitoring and evaluation needed a management information system that used quantitative indicators on inputs and outputs, beneficiary contact monitoring, diagnostic studies focused on implementation problems, and evaluation. The consensus culminated in the publication of two volumes (Casley and Kumar, 1987, 1988) under the joint auspices of the Food and Agriculture Organization, the International Fund for Agricultural Development, and the World Bank. These studies have been widely used in both bilateral and multilateral agencies. Recently, however, two major developments have emerged that might have significant implications for the monitoring and evaluation of ARD projects.

First, development experts have started constructing indicators that can provide a panoramic view of a sector and its subsectors. Such indicators are expected to assist policy and decision makers in formulating long-term strategies, identifying sectoral and subsectoral needs, and developing projects to meet those needs. The results of these efforts look promising. For example, following the recommendations of its Portfolio Management Task Force, the World Bank initiated interesting work on project-, sector-, and subsector-level key performance indicators (World Bank, 1994). Several of the indicators have been identified, and attempts are being made to refine and develop consensus around them. The goal is to issue a revised and generally accepted list of agricultural sector indicators in 1995. In addition, World Bank experts have identified indicators in many ARD subsectors such as irrigation, rural finance, forestry, extension, and livestock. Some of these are based on the experience of field staff and researchers; others are new. Considerable work is being done in the U.S. Agency for International Development (USAID) field offices on constructing sector- and subsector-level indicators. Such efforts will contribute to better monitoring and evaluation of development interventions.

Second, and undoubtedly more ambitious, is the effort to develop a comprehensive performance measurement system (PMS) based on quantitative indicators that can measure the collective performance of several projects in a sector or subsector. The unit of analysis is not a project but a sector- or subsector-level program that typically includes many projects implemented through different organizations and organizational units over a relatively long time period of ten to twelve years. Development experts are seeking to apply the PMS model to programs in developing countries. Much of this work is being done by private consulting firms that are experimenting with the PMS framework in USAID-supported development interventions. One such firm is Management Systems International, which has taken a leadership role in program performance measurement. The firm has developed a framework to analyze development programs, identified performance indicators, and provided consulting services to overseas USAID Missions. This chapter focuses on performance measurement at the program level and critically examines the applicability of the PMS model to ARD programs funded by international donors.

The scope of this chapter is limited in three ways. First, as mentioned above, the chapter does not examine the PMS model for a single project or intervention. Instead, it focuses on programs, which by definition are long-term, multiactivity, multisite endeavors that usually include many projects in a subsector. For example, all projects undertaken by an international donor agency on irrigation, agricultural extension and research, or rural finance in a country or group of countries constitute a program for the purpose of this discussion. (This distinction between a project and a program is somewhat unique to USAID. Other international agencies do not always make such a distinction.) Second, the discussion is restricted to only one PMS model—the model that seeks to measure results on the basis of a set of predetermined, quantifiable performance indicators. Finally, the chapter is written from the vantage point of international donor agencies rather than that of host countries or of intended beneficiaries.

The Performance Measurement System

The PMS model was invented in the early 1980s to improve the performance and cost-effectiveness of government services. Interest in PMS was strengthened by the highly visible report of the National Performance Review led by U.S. Vice President Al Gore, which—among other recommendations—outlined a performance measurement agenda for U.S. government agencies. Furthermore, the Government Performance and Results Act, which became law in 1993, made PMS a requirement in all U.S. federal agencies.

PMS is essentially a data collection and analysis system for measuring the performance of a program with reference to the program's stated objectives. It involves the following steps (Britan 1991; Cook, VanSant, Stewart, and Adrian, 1993; Gale 1994):

Analysis of the goals and objectives of the program, which should be measurable. Analysis includes development of strategic action plans that state clearly and precisely the objectives and anticipated program results to be achieved within a specified time. Many donor-funded development initiatives in the ARD sectors have clearly articulated goals, quantified targets, and workplans.

Identification of a set of indicators to measure performance. Indicators are defined as specific and objectively verifiable measures of change or results produced by an activity. They are invariably quantitative; even when the information is qualitative, it is presented numerically. Indicators can capture one or more dimensions of performance and results. Obviously, composite indexes that measure multidimensions are more difficult to construct and require more elaborate data collection than do simple indicators.

ARD interventions have a long record of developing, refining, and using a variety of indicators to measure output and impact. In fact, they are among the first to have used performance indicators. Since the late 1920s, the extension departments of U.S. land-grant universities had been using indicators to measure the diffusion and effects of agricultural innovations in the United States. When these institutions were asked to provide overseas technical assistance, they drew from their experience to develop indicators appropriate to the conditions of developing societies.

Establishment of a data-gathering system to collect indicator data from program records, surveys, agricultural censuses, and occasionally, direct observation methods. Invariably, such a system requires baselines against which future performance of outputs and outcomes is measured.

Analysis and interpretation of performance data and communication of the findings to program managers. A key assumption is that managers will be able and willing to make rational decisions in light of the information gathered. The onus is on management for the effective use of PMS.

Development Programs and Their Distinctive Settings

International development programs differ significantly from domestic programs in highly industrialized nations. Although the differences are often of degree, lighter versus darker gray, they have implications for the implementation of a performance measurement system. At least three such differences deserve special mention.

The evolving nature of development programs. Like many other development initiatives, ARD programs evolve over time and are, at their best, innovative and experimental. The targets, workplans, and even intervention strategies change during the life of a program. ARD programs learn from experience and constantly respond to unfolding events in unpredictable environments. As a result, the design documents and appraisal reports of the constituent projects seldom prove to be realistic blueprints for the proposed activities. In fact, as early as 1980, Korton (1980) distinguished between the blueprint and the process approach and suggested that participants consider the development process itself as a learning process.

Innovative development programs are more prone to change than those based on proven intervention models. For example, an evaluation of USAID agribusiness programs (Kumar, 1994) revealed that in the seven countries studied, programs gradually shifted their primary focus from domestic to foreign markets. Although domestic markets offered limited potential for high-value agroprocessing and marketing, international markets for nontraditional agricultural exports were opening up. Consequently, the programs redirected their resources to the promotion of nontraditional exports, which contributed to the programs' eventual success. An unintended consequence of this change was that the originally selected performance indicators for which data collection systems had been established no longer mirrored the performance of these programs.

Hence, the evolving nature of ARD programs imposes heavy demands on monitoring systems that are based on quantifiable indicators and targets. To be effective and relevant, such systems need to be able to revise or reformulate their initial indicators and baseline data. This is more easily said than done. Once a measurement system is established and indicators are selected, the system tends to take on a life of its own, irrespective of the changing direction of the program.

Limited organizational capabilities. Private and public organizations in most developing countries have limited organizational capabilities. Often, public sector organizations are more geared to "rent seeking" than to providing needed services efficiently and effectively. In many of the poorest countries, standards of accountability are minimal, if they exist. Concepts such as "managing for results" are unfamiliar, and the organizational culture of public-sector organizations, which host and manage program components, is rarely supportive of major management innovations. The situation is only slightly better in the private sector. Such conditions are prone to constrain the effective functioning and use of performance measurement systems. For example, the elaborate management information systems established in integrated rural development programs in the 1970s and early 1980s failed to make headway despite massive commitment of resources (Coleman, 1990, 1992).

Although the data collection and analysis capabilities of developing countries have vastly improved during the past two decades, much remains to be desired. Many countries, particularly in Africa, lack the institutional capacity to conduct sample surveys and to translate findings into meaningful operational and policy recommendations useful to management. When foreign experts are brought in for information gathering and analysis, the cost rises enormously, raising questions about the economic returns on such investments.

Conceptualizing results. Results are often conceptualized differently by the development community than by the exponents of performance measurement for domestic programs. The term "results" in the context of U.S. domestic programs usually refers to the immediate outputs of ongoing programs, for example, the decline in the cost of waste disposal as a result of privatization. The development community tends to go beyond such a short-term view of results by focusing on second- and even third-generation results. To explain the development community's concept of results, it is necessary to mention the simple causal logic underlying many development programs:

$$\text{Inputs} \longrightarrow \text{outputs} \longrightarrow \text{effects} \longrightarrow \text{impacts}$$

The *inputs* of human and material resources expended on development programs produce immediate *outputs*. For example, an extension program trains farmers in the use of a high-yielding variety of paddy or an agribusiness project finances the purchase of food-processing technology. These outputs in turn contribute to their own intermediate outcomes, which are often termed *effects*. For example, the training of farmers results in higher yields of paddy, or the technical assistance given to agribusiness firms improves their profitability. *Impacts* refers to the long-term outcomes or results of development programs on the people, economy, society, or environment. Outcomes of development interventions on per capita income, nutritional status, and economic growth rates are examples of impacts.

The essential point here is that when development experts discuss results, they tend to include the higher-order and longer-term effects and impacts. To them, the results are not only the immediate outputs of a program but also the intermediate effects and long-term impacts on the development of peoples, institutions, and economies. As indicated below, such a comprehensive conceptualization of results often aggravates measurement and data collection problems.

Methodological Issues

Before a PMS model can be effectively introduced in an ARD program, several methodological problems, outlined below, must be addressed. (The technical issues of validity, reliability, precision, equivalence, and aggregation of indicators are well covered in standard textbooks and are therefore not discussed here.)

Measuring Net Effects and Impacts. A critical, though not always explicit, assumption behind the PMS model is that a set of performance indicators can measure the results attributable to a program. Although this assumption may be correct when the focus is on outputs, it becomes doubtful when results are defined in terms of higher-order effects and impacts of programs. Only in a few cases can performance indicators alone assess the effects and impacts that have directly resulted from ARD programs and not from extraneous factors.

The textbook approach for measuring effects and impacts is to follow either of two methodological strategies: the quasi-experimental design or controlling for the effects of exogenous factors by statistical tools, particularly multiple regression analysis. Both approaches use a set of indicators, but extensive reviews of ARD projects show that neither approach has succeeded. ARD interventions have invariably failed to measure the "net impacts" of a project, much less of a more complex program. Even when serious attempts have been made, they have been based on heroic assumptions and questionable data.

Determining whether a program is producing the intended effects and impacts requires the following:

Time-series data on selected indicators. For example, a national agricultural extension program designed to increase cereal production requires production estimates for the geographical areas covered by the program.

A periodic reexamination of the key assumptions of the underlying intervention models. Reexamination is necessary because the settings and contents of programs evolve over time. The evaluators of the extension program, for example, must routinely reexamine assumptions about the efficacy of the technical packages and the delivery system to determine whether the assumptions are still justified.

Some evidence, not necessarily quantitative, to factor out the possibility of extraneous variables having largely produced the observed changes. Again, evaluators of the extension program should be able to establish from key informant interviews, previous studies, and direct observation methods whether or not the observed change in cereal production was largely attributable to nonprogram factors, such as an improved marketing system.

A carefully designed and judiciously implemented PMS model can in most cases generate time-series data on selected indicators, but it cannot adequately respond to the remaining two requirements, which usually require supplementary analyses. For those, evaluators may need to conduct in-depth evaluation studies to complement performance indicators in assessing attribution or in evaluating the continuing relevance of program outputs, targets, and objectives in a changing environment.

A caveat is necessary at this stage. When the causal relationships between program outputs, effects, and impacts are theoretically established beyond reasonable doubt, performance indicators can give a satisfactory indication of outcomes resulting from a program. Irrigation programs provide a good example. If the construction or rehabilitation of canals has brought additional land under intensive cultivation, evaluators can use simple econometric models to estimate the value of the additional production generated by the program.

Time Frame. The effects and impacts of an ARD program tend not to be visible early in the program's implementation. It can take years before performance becomes apparent and can be adequately measured by indicators. Even a simple trend in crop production attributable to an intervention may take years before it can be measured. Casley and Kumar (1987, p. 118) constructed a table that shows the number of years of high-quality data required to determine a distinct trend with a given level of accuracy and statistical confidence. Their calculations demonstrate that in order to detect a rising trend in production of 4 percent per time point, with an accuracy of 25 percent either side for 95 percent confidence, twenty-one points are required—equivalent to twenty-one years of data for annual cropping. After presenting different scenarios based on varying levels of the accepted margins of error and statistical confidence, they conclude that determining yield or production trends in rain-fed small farming areas may be impossible within the implementation period of most projects.

The example of rain-fed agriculture is not unique. In a wide range of ARD programs—from agroprocessing to infrastructure construction—results may take years to generate and are often influenced by unpredictable environments. Thus, evaluators often need outcome data for several time periods to assess performance trends. The implication is clear: PMS performance information on higher-order outcomes may not be of much immediate management use during the early implementation years. The case is entirely different when it comes to the use of PMS to monitor program inputs, outputs, and shorter-term or intermediate effects. These factors can be measured regularly during the early stages of implementation and the information used to guide management decisions early on.

Using Sector-Level Indicators for Performance Measurement. As the term indicates, sector-level indicators measure changes in an entire sector of an economy. Gross agricultural production, agricultural production as a fraction of gross national product, agricultural productivity, volume of agricultural exports or value of output per hectare are examples of agricultural sector-level indicators.

Sector-wide indicators are often used in ARD programs to measure performance, even when the programs do not cover the entire country or are limited to a specific subsector. Such practice is commonly justified for three reasons. First, the purpose of all programs is to improve the performance of a sector. Thus the use of sector-level indicators is considered appropriate. After all, extension programs are designed and implemented to increase agricultural production. Second, many if not most ARD interventions are designed to introduce new ideas, approaches, and technologies. They tend to generate "externalities" that are not necessarily confined to the subsector or to the geographic areas covered by the intervention. For example, the experience of many countries in which the green revolution in wheat succeeded demonstrated that when farmers saw the technical and economic viability of high-yield variety seeds, the use of the new variety spread well beyond the initial program area. Finally, the use of sectoral indicators is advocated because such data are widely available and thus can be easily used.

Although these arguments have some validity, the use of sectoral indicators is often questionable. The strategy suffers from a basic flaw in that it typically violates an essential requirement—that an indicator be sensitive to intervention-induced changes. The causal links between an ARD program that is limited in geographic range or in scope and observed changes at the sectoral level tend to be remote and weak. Under these conditions, changes in the dependent variables might have little or nothing to do with the intervention itself. For example, an agribusiness promotion program in a Central American country used the volume of nontraditional agricultural exports as a performance indicator. Because the country registered significant growth in nontraditional exports, the program was considered a resounding success. An in-depth analysis of the program's technical assistance, however, showed that the firms that largely accounted for the exports did not receive much assistance. In this particular case, the observed rapid growth in nontraditional agricultural exports was not induced by the program, yet the program received credit because of the use of sector-level indicators (Kumar, 1994). A reverse scenario—a program is considered a failure even when it has performed well—is also possible.

In summary, a PMS model based on inappropriate sector-level indicators cannot provide realistic feedback to managers and policy planners. It therefore cannot serve the accountability function that is its primary function.

Limits to Quantification. The PMS model primarily if not exclusively uses quantitative indicators. Although a growing set of quantitative indicators for many subsectors in agriculture has been developed and is now in use, the status of indicators in agricultural research, rural community development, agroprocessing, and marketing is uncertain. Many questions of reliability and validity still remain. The point to be emphasized here is that most available indicators focus on inputs and outputs, not on the results of ARD programs.

A basic limitation of an information system based solely on quantitative indicators lies in the simple fact that not all important factors, conditions, outputs, effects, and impacts of a program can be easily quantified. Information relating to staff morale, political environment, links with external institutions, factors affecting performance, and even economic externalities are very difficult to quantify. Much information—often the most relevant—is lost in the quantification process. Thus, a PMS system may provide a distorted picture if it concentrates on what is measurable and overlooks what cannot be quantified.

Data Collection and Analysis. Although data on inputs and outputs of ARD programs can be gathered largely from program records and documents, much more elaborate efforts are needed to conduct key informant interviews, minisurveys, and the like to gather information on the effects and impacts of programs. In most cases, performance information for higher-order objectives can be collected only through multisite, longitudinal sample surveys, but such surveys are expensive and time-consuming when conducted in the rural areas of developing societies, and the survey data often are inaccurate.

The experience of conducting large-scale surveys for development programs has been dismal. Most observers agree that the large-scale data collection efforts enthusiastically launched during the 1970s and 1980s frequently failed to generate reliable and timely information, resulting in a colossal waste of resources (for example Casley and Kumar 1987, 1988; Coleman 1990, 1992; Kumar 1987, 1993). A number of persistent problems typically plagued large-scale surveys. (1) In the absence of an analytical framework, variables were inappropriately identified and poorly conceptualized. In their enthusiasm for comprehensiveness, survey designers often weighed their design with too many independent, intervening, and dependent variables resulting in costly and unrealistic designs. (2) Little attention was given to making the concepts operational, and the issue of validity of indicator definitions was largely ignored. (3) In many instances, sampling procedures were basically flawed. The sample was unnecessarily large, creating data-gathering and management problems. (4) The large sample size, poor training of enumerators, and inadequate supervision resulted in high nonsampling errors, leading to dubious findings. (5) In most instances, surveys were not completed in time. Initial enthusiasm evaporated after the baseline survey, and follow-up surveys were often not undertaken at all. (6) Even when the data were gathered, they were not analyzed in time. Usually, raw data were presented to the stakeholders without analysis. No attempts were made to translate the findings into concrete recommendations for action. (7) Under these conditions, managers simply ignored the findings even when they were communicated to them. Consequently, other than providing employment for some expatriate consultants, the surveys produced no return on investment.

These failures should not lead donors to conclude that such efforts will never work. Experience and lessons learned can improve the way future sample surveys are conducted. The past failures, however, should alert evaluators to the magnitude of the tasks and the seriousness of the risks involved. They also point to the significant commitment of human and material resources needed to undertake large surveys. Even then, there is no assurance that a survey will generate the type of performance information on results needed for program and policy decision making.

Reification of Performance Indicators. The tendency of program staff to reify performance indicators poses a management problem for PMS systems. Instead of treating indicators as measures, program staff tend to view indicators as the outcomes of the program themselves, often distorting the program's true objectives in the process. Their attitude is similar to that of students who measure the success of their education by the grades they receive. For example, agricultural extension staff commonly include nonfarming women in training courses to inflate the indicator used to measure women's participation. To prove their efforts successful, experts in agribusiness projects are inclined to channel technical assistance to largely successful firms, even though such firms often do not need assistance. In the process, firms and entrepreneurs struggling to survive are ignored. Because of the pressure to meet targets, family planning workers are known to provide pills to women who have passed their childbearing age. The problem of reification is not insurmountable, however, and can be addressed with the use of multiple indicators and qualitative studies, as well as adequate supervision.

Concluding Observations

The purpose of this discussion is not to imply that the PMS model can never work. Instead, the message is to caution the development community about the extreme care needed in designing the system, selecting the indicators, and developing the strategies for gathering the needed data. Specialists should examine the distinctive needs and landscapes of the developing world and determine the types of modifications needed when applying the PMS model. Above all, they should be realistic in their expectations, recognizing the limitations and shortcomings of the PMS model for ARD programs. This chapter proposes the following as next steps:

First, the PMS system should be designed with a focus on monitoring program performance equally at all levels—inputs, outputs, effects, and impacts. Too great a focus on higher-level outcomes creates many conceptual and methodological problems that are not easily solved. Evaluators need to pay more attention to identifying and measuring intermediate outcomes that are amenable to progress in the shorter term and yet can get beyond immediate program outputs. Leading and proxy indicators of results that take advantage of lower cost and more practical data collection techniques need greater exploration as well.

Second, tracking the results of ARD programs requires a much more comprehensive approach to monitoring and evaluation than is typical of many PMS models (Binnendijk and Gale, 1994; Cook, VanSant, Stewart, and Adrian, 1994). Casley and Kumar (1987) propose that an effective project monitoring and evaluation system include (1) a management information system based on indicators, (2) beneficiary contact monitoring to understand the response of target groups, (3) diagnostic studies to identify practical solutions to implementation problems, and (4) process and impact evaluations. Such a comprehensive approach can serve the decision needs of a variety of stakeholders. There is no reason why this framework cannot be applied at the program level.

Finally, further research, particularly systematic analysis of past experience, is urgently needed. Such research should focus on the issues of measurement, validity, and reliability of performance indicators; participatory approaches to data collection and analysis; low-cost data collection strategies; incentive strategies for promoting a sense of ownership among program stakeholders; and the implications of the construct of a "learning organization" as it relates to monitoring and evaluation. USAID is currently developing PRISM (Performance Measurement Information for Strategic Measurement), which is grappling with similar issues. The World Bank's Key Performance Indicators is also attempting to address these problems. Such attempts, it is hoped, will help further clarify these issues, develop more sophisticated analytical frameworks, and identify promising paths for the future.

References

Binnendijk, A., and Gale, S. "Performance Measurement in USAID: The PRISM System." *USAID Evaluation News*, 1994, 6 (1).

Britan, G. M. "Measuring Program Performance for Federal Agencies: Issues and Options for Performance Indicators." Washington, D.C.: U.S. Agency for International Development, 1991.

Casley, D. J., and Kumar, K. *Project Monitoring and Evaluation in Agriculture*. Baltimore, Md.: Johns Hopkins University Press for the World Bank, 1987.

Casley, D. J., and Kumar, K. *The Collection, Analysis and Use of Monitoring and Evaluation Data*. Baltimore, Md.: Johns Hopkins University Press for the World Bank, 1988.

Coleman, G. "Problems in Project Level Monitoring and Evaluation: Lessons from One Major Agency." *Journal of Agricultural Economics*, 1990, 41.

Coleman, G. "Monitoring and Evaluation in Agricultural and Rural Development Projects." *Journal of International Development*, 1992, 4 (5).

Cook, T. J., VanSant, J., Stewart, L., and Adrian, J. *Performance Measurement: Lessons Learned*. Research Triangle Park, N.C.: Research Triangle Institute, 1993.

Gale, S. "Performance Measurement: Public Pressures and Legislative Mandates." *USAID Evaluation News*, 1994, 6 (1).

Korton, D. C. "Community Organization and Rural Development: A Learning Process Approach." *Public Administration Review*, 1980, 40 (5).

Kumar, K. *Impact Indicators: Critical Issues*. Washington D.C.: U.S. Agency for International Development, 1987.

Kumar, K. (ed.). *Rapid Appraisal Methods*. Washington D.C.: World Bank, 1993.

Kumar, K. *Generating Broad-Based Growth through Agribusiness Promotion: Assessment of USAID Experience*. Washington D.C.: U.S. Agency for International Development, 1994.

World Bank, Operations Evaluation Department (OED). "An Overview of Monitoring and Evaluation in the World Bank." Washington, D.C.: World Bank, 1994.

KRISHNA KUMAR is a senior analyst at the Center for Development Information and Evaluation in the U.S. Agency for International Development.

The nature of performance criteria and the timing of evaluation are crucial determinants of the relevance and accuracy of findings for education and training systems. The author proposes specific indicators adapted to different evaluation situations and stresses the importance of conducting ex ante and impact rather than just input evaluations.

Using Evaluation Indicators to Track the Performance of Education Programs

George Psacharopoulos

As private demand for schooling at all levels increases and the ability of governments to finance it decreases, the evaluation of education and training systems gains in importance. However, evaluation in education means different things to different people. It can be "back of the envelope," descriptive, or analytical, and it can use a variety of methodologies and indicators. This chapter focuses on education *programs*, which have a broader reach than the traditional education project financed by donor organizations and include such intangibles as policy change. The chapter is concerned with the evaluation of *public* education systems because, by definition, private schools have a built-in self-evaluation component: unless they somehow satisfy their customers, they cannot survive. The thrust of the chapter is to demonstrate the importance of tracking the performance of educational programs continuously, rather than to conduct one overall evaluation at the end of the program.

Education programs present special problems for the evaluator. First is the issue of lead time. It takes several years to build a school, several more years of student attendance at that school, and many more years thereafter before graduates reach the labor market. At what stage can evaluators legitimately assess the program and pronounce it good or bad?

Second, comparing different education levels and types also poses problems. For example, can evaluators apply the same evaluation criteria to both primary education and vocational schools?

Third, in recent years, education programs have typically included several components, such as physical construction, textbook production and distribution, policy change, and institutional strengthening. All three components aim to accomplish the same grand result—to contribute to economic growth and poverty alleviation in a particular country. But how can each component be evaluated separately?

Fourth, partly for ethical reasons, education is the sector least amenable to experimental design, especially in the case of entry to different types of schools (although experimental design is possible for evaluating learning processes and materials). How then can evaluators establish a valid control group for evaluation purposes?

Fifth, because nearly everyone has had some exposure to education, it is easy to assume that a good school can be differentiated from a bad one (Newsweek, 1991). How can evaluators resist this intuitive logic and evaluate according to scientific criteria? More specifically, there are at least two classes of evaluation: descriptive and analytical (for an elaboration, see Psacharopoulos, 1994a). The first is mainly based on opinions and impressions obtained from visiting schools. The second is more demanding and requires extensive surveys and the use of statistical techniques. Although descriptive evaluations are expedient and relatively cheap, how valid are they?

Finally, the far-reaching benefits often associated with education programs cannot be easily summarized using specific project objectives such as equity and efficiency. The intended benefits also may have little to do with public investment objectives such as growth and equity. For example, a government's objectives for investing in an education program may be politically motivated, and these public policy objectives change over time. As objectives are realized and are changed, the original outcome of the program may no longer be desired. Evaluators then need to focus on which objectives really guide investments by governments and parents and then to ensure that the outcomes selected accurately measure these objectives.

The discussion that follows addresses these questions and offers a set of evaluation indicators that might prove useful in tracking education program performance.

The Evaluation Quandary

Consider a typical education project in the context of any school cycle lasting six years (Figure 6.1). Assume that the project was conceived in 1980 and that it takes ten years for it to reach a point at which it can be evaluated: one year for it to be justified, three years to build the physical facilities and put other components in place, and six years for the first students to graduate. In addition to building the schools, the project components include producing textbooks, revising the curricula, institutionally strengthening the ministry of education, and instituting fees in higher education. The project was justified on grounds that it would contribute to the country's economic growth, alleviate poverty, improve school quality, and supply the labor market with badly needed vital skills.

Figure 6.1. Project Phases and Evaluator Points of Entry

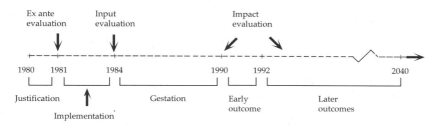

Consider, as an illustration, Indonesia's First Education Project. The project was to create five technical training centers, each serving nearby senior secondary schools. It was approved in October 1970 and closed in March 1977. Audits conducted by the World Bank in 1980, however, judged that it was too early to evaluate the project, that is, to determine the employability of the graduates, ten years after the project was approved by the bank's executive directors.

As Figure 6.1 illustrates, the evaluator can enter the picture at three main points in the time sequence of an education program: (1) at the end of the justification process, and even before project construction begins (referred to as *ex ante evaluation* in this chapter); (2) at the end of the implementation process (*input evaluation*); and (3) at the end of the gestation process (usually called *impact evaluation*). The majority of so-called "education evaluations" refer to input evaluation. The reason is simple: evaluation at this stage seems logical and convenient. Impact evaluations also are conducted but only rarely, and the author knows of no one who conducts ex ante evaluation of the kind advocated in this chapter.

Ex Ante Evaluation. At its conception, every education program is justified on the basis of a set of criteria or program objectives (Table 6.1). Typical rationales for justifying a project are the project's contribution to enhancing productivity leading to economic growth and poverty alleviation. Increasingly, improving overall literacy has become a rationale, as have employment generation and meeting critical skill shortages in the economy. Improving school quality and increasing access for minority groups also can be objectives. Institutional strengthening, with the goal of improving the ability of the education ministry to manage and monitor the system, is another common objective.

In an ex ante evaluation an independent entity assesses the validity of the education program's foundations. Such an assessment has to be undertaken by someone other than the person or organization sponsoring or justifying the project; the sponsor would assume the program was valid and would meet its objectives.

As often happens in the nonexact sciences, an education program is justified based on intuitive assumptions about its eventual effects. Although

Table 6.1. Justification Criteria and Ex Ante Evaluation Indicators

Justification Criteria/ Project Objective	Indicator
Economic/productivity growth	Results of previous impact evaluation studies
Poverty alleviation	Program beneficiaries by socioeconomic background
Employment generation	Nondistortionary macro policies
Meeting skill shortages	Findings of previous tracer study placements
Institutional strengthening	Incentives structure

evidence may exist—for example, from past evaluations or research—sponsors may not take the evidence into account, proceeding to implement a program that could prove ineffective in practice. For example, an education project has been justified on the grounds that it will help meet the country's shortages in some critical skills. The likely impact of a program with such rationale already could be discounted, even before the relevant vocational schools are built. Even if the supply of the specialists (for example, agricultural specialists) increases, there is no reason to expect that graduates will actually work in that sector—as two research and analytical evaluations of World Bank projects have sadly shown (Psacharopoulos and Loxley, 1985).

Moreover, if the program included a higher education project on the grounds that it would promote economic growth, evidence might have shown that a primary education project could contribute more to growth in that country, given the overwhelming literature indicating that the rate of return to investments in primary education is higher than the returns to university education (for a review of such evidence, see Psacharopoulos, 1994b). If the higher education project was justified on the grounds of poverty alleviation, it could be argued that building another university would likely increase disparities in the country rather than assist those who are poor and illiterate to increase their earnings.

A program justified on the basis of employment creation will need to have in place an appropriate macroeconomic framework that avoids domestic and international distortions (policies seemingly unrelated to education) before it can succeed. Similarly, if a program objective is to strengthen and reform a country's educational institutions, proper incentives need to have been established before the program can achieve its goal.

Two reasons explain why myopia at the program justification stage can lead education programs into blind alleys. First, programs are justified based on intuitive logic, often without the backing of scientific evidence. Second, the people justifying the project are often unaware of or simply too busy to absorb the latest research and evaluation findings on the subject. (For example, it was not long ago that education projects in a major sponsoring agency were justified by architects.)

Input Evaluation. This is the easy part of the evaluation process, but because it is so easy compared with other methods, evaluation often stops after this stage. Table 6.2 shows typical "evaluation" indicators for the implementation stage. The indicators are straightforward, factual, and involve either descriptive or accounting questions that can be answered at the end of program implementation.

Although such input evaluations should not be used in lieu of a true impact evaluation, they can provide useful intermediate feedback to policy makers. If a project includes high-quality evaluation components that are conscientiously implemented, the uncertainty of benefit reestimates will likely be reduced. As argued below, input evaluation is a necessary part of a full program evaluation, but by itself, it is not adequate.

Impact Evaluation. This most demanding type of evaluation presents unique design and measurement obstacles—hence its rarity. Because of the timing sequence mentioned earlier (and shown in Figure 6.1), several years, if not decades, must pass before an impact evaluation can begin. Also, unless a control group is included in the education program, establishing the base of the evaluation becomes extremely difficult and is likely to be inaccurate. Few education programs at their inception include the collection of baseline data, and without baseline data, later comparisons of the effects of the program on participants versus effects of the absence of the program on the control groups become difficult.

Impact evaluation was used to evaluate diversified secondary schools in Colombia and Tanzania. Evaluators not only gathered data on diversified schools and their graduates but also polled general secondary schools to assess the differential incremental effects, if any, of the project graduates relative to

Table 6.2. Project Components and Input Evaluation Indicators

Component	Indicator
School construction	Have schools been constructed according to architectural norms?
Textbook production/revision	Does every student have a book?
Curriculum revision	Do textbooks reflect new curricula?
Resource allocation	Has the money allocated to the project been disbursed?
University fees	Has the appropriate law been passed?

the control group graduates. But the work was classified as "research" rather than impact evaluation and was thus nearly ignored by traditional evaluators. (For other World Bank impact evaluations, see Jamison, Searle, Heyneman, and Galda, 1981, on radio programs in Nicaragua; Mayo, Hornik, and McAnany, 1976, on El Salvador's instructional television; and Harbison and Hanushek, 1992, on primary education in Northeast Brazil.)

Table 6.3 lists the most crucial criteria and measurement indicators for impact evaluations. These are divided into three clusters: learning related, equity and poverty related, and labor market related, roughly corresponding to the time sequence during which they can be measured. (For an expanded discussion of impact evaluation indicators, see Oakes, 1989, and Berk, 1984.)

The learning indicator refers to the achievement gain of the students graduating from the schools included in the program. It should be emphasized that achievement in this context refers to the *value added* relative to the cohort of students in question rather than the absolute achievement of the entire graduating class. The tool for making such evaluations is an educational production function that standardizes for the host of characteristics (other than school related) that can affect achievement. (For a review and results of such functions, see Hanushek, 1986, for the United States, and Fuller, 1986, for developing countries.)

Even if the educational achievement of students has increased, it is necessary to assess the cost at which the increase was realized. This is referred to in the literature as costing the coefficients of an educational production function. (For an application to Brazil, see Harbison and Hanushek, 1992.) Juxtaposing the achievement gain of students against the cost of realizing it can lead to some unexpected conclusions, for example, that school buildings do not matter as much as textbooks and writing materials.

Another indicator for impact evaluation is determining who gained access to the school. If poverty alleviation is the main justification for the program,

Table 6.3. Impact Evaluation Criteria and Indicators

Criteria	Indicator
Learning	
Incremental learning	Achievement gain
Cost-effectiveness of learning	Achievement gain per dollar spent
Equity/poverty	
Access to school	Attendance by socioeconomic background
Incidence of benefits and costs	Who pays and who benefits?
Labor market	
Graduates' employability	Tracer study placements
Graduates' productivity	Earnings in the private sector
Cost/benefit analysis	Graduate earnings in relation to the control group (rate of return)

which socioeconomic group benefited most? Did more of the students come from financially better-off backgrounds or from poorer backgrounds? Also, who paid what to attend the school? If the program includes university education, the incidence of the costs and benefits and attendance rates by socioeconomic background are the key evaluation indicators.

For education programs with labor market objectives, a tracer study of the graduates is the only valid tool for evaluating impact. (For a review, see Psacharopoulos and Hinchliffe, forthcoming.) A questionnaire distributed to the graduates immediately after they leave school and again a couple of years after graduation records whether they have found a job, how long it took them to find that job, whether the job relates to what they learned in school (essential information for evaluating vocational programs), the economic sector in which they work (public, private), and their earnings. The incremental earnings of members of a control group that did not attend the program school can be used to calculate a rate of return on the investment.

Consider, as an example, Indonesia's Second Education Project, the objective of which was to provide training for middle-level agricultural workers. The project was rated "good" on the grounds that enrollment targets were met, but a World Bank audit found that because a tracer study was not conducted, accurate information on the type of employment found by the program's graduates was not available.

Calculations of rates of return have led to some counterintuitive conclusions, namely that primary education has a higher social rate of return than the other levels of education, that general secondary education is more profitable than vocational education, and that investment in women's education is more profitable than that for men. (For a global review of recent rate of return estimates and a discussion of the controversies surrounding this topic, see Psacharopoulos, 1994b.)

Evaluation Methodology and Indicators by Education Level and Type. The most appropriate evaluation tool for impact evaluation depends on the education level on which the program operates (see Table 6.4). For primary education projects, cost-effectiveness will suffice. Because many educated women will never work in the formal labor market, trying to trace their earnings twenty years later is pointless. However, tracing can be used for assessing program effects on working women, for example, to determine the extent of gender discrimination in a given economy.

Moving up the education ladder, cost-effectiveness continues to be used for evaluation in secondary education. In some countries secondary education is becoming nearly compulsory, so it has to be evaluated regardless of labor market outcomes. But when a secondary vocational education program is justified on the grounds of rectifying skill shortages or increasing the productivity of graduates, cost/benefit analysis must be done, and, as already mentioned, such studies have led to some unexpected conclusions.

Cost-effectiveness can be used to evaluate university education, especially if the provision of mass social science programs (to expediently satisfy the demand for higher education) is an objective. But when the rationale of the program is to achieve a labor market outcome, cost/benefit analysis is necessary. A postsecondary, nonuniversity technical college education that costs $20,000 per student may require an astronomical increase in the graduates' productivity over the control group to yield an acceptable rate of return. In such a case, a competent ex ante evaluation would have aborted such a project even before the first brick was laid.

Evaluation Credibility. The different types of evaluation described above have different degrees of credibility (see Table 6.5). Input and ex ante evaluations provide only a necessary condition, or just one element, of a complete evaluation of an education program. The fact that program money was disbursed and schools built does not mean that the program fulfilled its objectives, especially when objectives relate to remote labor market outcomes. Only an impact evaluation can provide a sufficient condition or definitive evaluation of the program. However, given the long time period necessary before a true impact evaluation can be carried out and the need for timely decisions on education programs being prepared, program sponsors should give greater attention to ex ante evaluation. Although by itself ex ante evaluation offers only one element of a complete evaluation, it can help program preparers avoid disasters before they materialize.

Table 6.4. Most Appropriate Evaluation Tool by Education Level and Type

Education Level/Type	Evaluation Tool
Primary	Cost-effectiveness
Secondary general	Cost-effectiveness, cost/benefit
Secondary vocational	Cost/benefit
Vocational Training	Cost/benefit
University	Cost-effectiveness, cost/benefit

Table 6.5. Evaluation Types and Credibility Conditions

Evaluation Type	Credibility Condition
Ex ante	Necessary
Input evaluation	Necessary
Impact evaluation	Sufficient

International or Within-Country Comparisons?

International comparisons are popular indicators for both justifying and evaluating education programs, but they are often misleading. Examples of common comparisons among countries are enrollment ratios, share of education expenditure in the state budget or gross domestic product (GDP), education expenditure per student, or achievement scores.

Enrollment ratios for all levels of education, especially at the tertiary level, differ widely among countries. Moreover, the enrollment ratio of a country is the result of a very complex set of historical, cultural, and economic factors that cannot be replicated in another country in the short time span of an education program. It is therefore wrong to say that because one country has an education enrollment ratio of 20 percent for 18 to 24 year olds and another, less economically well-off country has only a ratio of 10 percent, the poorer country should raise its enrollment ratio to 20 percent as well. Also, in the poorer country, higher education might not be the most appropriate investment priority, given that other levels of education produce higher social returns.

International comparisons are often made of enrollments in the vocational stream of secondary education. The intuitive logic is that countries with a higher share of vocational students will do better economically because of the closer relevance of the curriculum to the world of work. Statistics from the former Soviet Union have repeatedly been cited as targets for southern European countries to reach. Yet, as recent history has shown, the intense vocationalization of secondary education in the former socialist countries has not made their economies perform better.

Germany, Japan, and Sweden are often cited as examples of countries with good vocational education and training programs, but, again, the strong economic performance of these countries cannot be attributed to the quality of their vocational training. These countries were able to afford such training, whereas today, the poorer countries that tend to imitate them might have different investment priorities if they use another justification criterion (for example, cost/benefit analysis) instead of international comparisons.

Another international comparison commonly referred to is the proportion of public resources devoted to education (as a share of the budget or GDP). Thus, if a country spends only 9 percent of its public budget on education, the argument states that it should be spending 15 percent because other countries do. At least two problems occur in this reasoning. First, as evidenced in detailed case studies, what matters is not the total amount of resources spent on education but how the money is spent (Hanushek, 1981). Second, such comparisons do not take into consideration the very significant education expenditures made by the private sector, another statistic that varies enormously between countries. Actually, taking this last factor into account, and given the inefficiency and inequity under which most state education systems operate, a low *public* expenditure on education might be a good indicator denoting efficiency in the use of resources or indicating that the private sector bears a great part of the country's total financial burden for education.

Another important gauge of how well or badly a given amount of public spending serves efficiency and equity is the share of such expenditure allocated to higher education. For example, a relatively poor country with high illiteracy and low-quality primary education spends 15 percent of its public budget on education, one third of which goes for higher education. In such a case, the higher share spent on education as a whole should not be considered an exemplary indicator for another country to adopt.

The same argument applies to comparisons of per student expenditure, usually given in constant U.S. dollars. Dramatic differences exist in per student expenditures between members of the Organization for Economic Cooperation and Development (OECD) and developing countries. But are OECD expenditures (even if expressed in constant purchasing power parity dollars) comparable to those in African countries? Perhaps a given amount of constant dollars will buy more educational services (of the same quality?) in Africa than in Europe.

Possibly the most impressionistic education indicator that has received much publicity in the international press, and especially in the United States, is student achievement (see Stevenson and Stigler, 1992; International Association for the Evaluation of Education Achievement, 1989; Lapointe, Mead, and Phillips, 1989; Lapointe, Mead, and Askew, 1992). Headlines often announce that U.S. students lag far behind their counterparts in Asian countries. According to the Science II study of the International Association for the Evaluation of Education Achievement (IEA), Papua, New Guinea, secondary school students perform at nearly the same level as their U.S. peers (Postlethwaite and Wiley, 1992). Yet careful reading of the footnotes of the original studies reveals that the Papua, New Guinea, students are one year older than their American peers and the country has a much more selective system of secondary education, whereas in the United States, more than 90 percent of the relevant age group attend high school. (See also U.S. Department of Education, 1983. For the controversy surrounding the validity of international achievement comparisons, see Husén, 1983; Rotberg, 1990; and Bradburn, Haertel, Schwille, and Torney-Purta, 1991.)

A Plea for Within-Country Comparisons. Educational research and evaluation need variation in order to establish cause and effect. International comparisons are difficult to make, however, because countries differ in so many respects other than in the education program under evaluation. How, for example, can evaluators control for different social attitudes in Asian and European countries, as reflected in, for example, the number of hours students spend watching television or the hours they devote to homework?

A more valid source of data variation for evaluation purposes comes from observing differences of a particular indicator in a country. In this way, the many unmeasurable, extraneous effects of intercountry differences are filtered out. Within-country, over-time comparisons are a better alternative to international comparisons. Evaluations that combine over-time comparisons (to establish the effect of the education program over a control group) and individual student and graduate comparisons are, of course, the most valid (as in Bishop, 1989, and Keeves, 1992).

Conclusion

The choice of method for evaluating education programs is not a matter of academic interest: it has profound practical applications. Depending on the type of evaluation used, the results can vary dramatically. For example, not until a research-level evaluation was conducted on diversified secondary school projects in Colombia and Tanzania did the World Bank stop lending for this kind of education. If traditional evaluation methods relying on the fulfillment of enrollment targets had been used, such schools would have been considered valid and funding would have continued.

Hundreds of possible indicators and several methods can be used for evaluating education programs. For example, a World Bank audit of Morocco's Education Sector Reform Program contained 159 monitoring indicators, yet none of them measured the unit cost of the interventions.

The most crucial, although least common, indicators needed for the proper evaluation of education programs are (1) cost per student by education level and curriculum type; (2) incidence of who pays and who benefits from public educational expenditure; (3) within-country achievement scores, by grade and subject (without attempting comparability among countries but building time trends of achievement within countries); (4) tracer information on how the output of the school system fits into the world of work (earnings of graduates by educational level, incidence of unemployment, length of time for recent graduates to find employment); and (5) incentives structure for program sustainability, for example, a merit pay system.

Methodologies for consideration include integrating impact evaluation early in the project cycle for control group definition; incorporating randomization as much as possible (for some examples on how to do this, see Newman, Rawlings, and Gertler, 1994); and above all, even before the program starts, thoroughly reviewing the evaluation and research literature on the primary aim of the program.

Finally, although only impact evaluations will provide conclusive, comprehensive information about the success or failure of a program, the results may not be particularly relevant for decision making. Circumstances change, and this feedback may not be as useful as concurrent evaluation results. Ex ante evaluations are highly relevant for decision making purposes, but this method is based primarily on conjecture. The resulting information may be incomplete. There is, consequently, a trade-off between relevance and accuracy imposed by the timing of the evaluation.

References

Berk, R. A. *A Guide to Criterion-Referenced Test Construction.* Baltimore, Md.: Johns Hopkins University Press, 1984.

Bishop, J. H. "Is the Test Score Decline Responsible for the Productivity Growth Decline?" *American Economic Review,* 1989, *79* (1), 178–197.

Bradburn, N., Haertel, E., Schwille, J., and Torney-Purta, J. "A Rejoinder to 'I Never Promised You First Place.'" *Phi Delta Kappan,* June 1991, 774–777.

Fuller, B. *Raising School Quality in Developing Countries: What Investments Boost Learning?* Washington, D.C.: World Bank, 1986.

Hanushek, E. "Throwing Money at Schools." *Journal of Policy Analysis and Management,* 1981, *1* (1), 19–41.

Hanushek, E. "The Economics of Schooling: Production and Efficiency in Public Schools." *Journal of Economic Literature,* 1986, *24,* 1141–77.

Harbison, R., and Hanushek, E. *Educational Performance of the Poor: Lessons from Rural Northeast Brazil.* London: Oxford University Press, 1992.

Husén, T. "Are Standards in U.S. Schools Really Lagging Behind Those in Other Countries?" *Phi Delta Kappan,* Mar. 1983, 455–461.

International Association for the Evaluation of Education Achievement (IEA). *The Underachieving Curriculum: Assessing U.S. Mathematics from an International Perspective.* Champaign, Ill.: Stipes, 1989.

Jamison, D., Searle, B., Heyneman, S. P., and Galda, K. *Improving Elementary Mathematics Education in Nicaragua: An Experimental Study of the Impact of Textbooks and Radio on Achievement.* Washington, D.C.: World Bank, 1981.

Keeves, J. P. *Learning Science in a Changing World.* The Hague: International Association for the Evaluation of Education Achievement, 1992.

Lapointe, A. E., Mead, N. A., and Askew, J. M. *Learning Mathematics.* Princeton, N.J.: Educational Testing Service, 1992.

Lapointe, A. E., Mead, N. A., and Phillips, G. W. *A World of Differences: An International Assessment of Mathematics and Science.* Princeton, N.J.: Educational Testing Service, 1989.

Mayo J., Hornik, R., and McAnany, E. *Educational Reform with Television: The El Salvador Experience.* Stanford, Calif.: Stanford University Press, 1976.

Newman, J., Rawlings, L., and Gertler, P. "Using Randomized Control Designs in Evaluating Social Sector Programs in Developing Countries." *World Bank Research Observer,* 1994, *9* (2), 181–201.

Newsweek. "The Best Schools in the World." *Newsweek,* Dec. 2, 1991.

Oakes, J. "What Educational Indicators? The Case for Assessing the School Context." *Educational Evaluation and Policy Analysis,* 1989, *11* (2), 181–199.

Postlethwaite, T. N., and Wiley, D. E. *The IEA Study of Science II: Science Achievement in Twenty-Three Counties.* Pergamon, 1992.

Psacharopoulos, G. "Evaluation of Education and Training: What Room for the Comparative Approach?" *International Review of Education,* 1994a, *40* (6).

Psacharopoulos, G. "Returns to Education: A Global Update." *World Development,* 1994b, 22 (9).

Psacharopoulos, G., and Hinchliffe, K. "Tracer Study Guidelines." *Journal of Educational Planning and Administration* (forthcoming).

Psacharopoulos, G., and Loxley, W. *Diversified Secondary Education and Development: Evidence from Colombia and Tanzania.* Baltimore, Md.: Johns Hopkins University Press, 1985.

Rotberg, I. "I Never Promised You First Place." *Phi Delta Kappan,* Dec. 1990, 296–303.

Stevenson, H. W., and Stigler, J. W. *The Learning Gap.* New York: Summit Books, 1992.

U.S. Department of Education, National Commission on Excellence in Education. *A Nation at Risk: The Imperative for Educational Reform.* Washington, D.C.: U.S. Government Printing Office, 1983.

GEORGE PSACHAROPOULOS *is senior adviser in human resources and operations policy of the World Bank.*

The recent shift in focus from "Women in Development" to "Gender and Development" has resulted in changes in the evaluation practices of development agencies. Although most of the indicators used to assess the gender impact of programs and projects still measure implementation progress rather than outcomes, a rich arsenal of techniques is available to enhance the impact of evaluation on the gender dimension of development.

Evaluating Gender Impacts

Caroline O. N. Moser

In "people centered" development, would evaluation procedures automatically incorporate a consideration of gender? This chapter highlights the importance of deliberate attention to evaluating the impact of development initiatives on people of different gender. After reviewing conceptual frameworks for evaluating gender impacts, it emphasizes the importance of clarity about what is to be measured—inputs or outcomes—and reviews recent experience and current initiatives with a bearing on the choice of evaluation methods and indicators.

Background

In development practice, "putting people first" (Cernea, 1985) has been neither automatic nor systematic. Even today, a large number of evaluations are not "peopled," and those that are do not necessarily distinguish people by gender. In the 1960s, economic development models of accelerated growth prioritized large infrastructure and industrial projects and focused on physical and financial progress, measured using indicators of financial and economic returns. In the 1970s, concern with basic needs, and the associated resource allocations to agriculture and the provision of basic physical and social services, targeted people as beneficiaries at the household level (Hicks and Streeten, 1979). Difficulties were soon encountered, not only in assigning a monetary value to social benefits but also in applying rate of return methodologies to deal with equity and distributional issues (Binnendijk, 1990; Cassen and associates, 1986).

From the 1970s onward, development debates broadened to include both economic and social objectives, with communities, households, and individual men, women, and children identified as participants in, rather than beneficiaries of, development. Noneconomic monitoring and evaluation techniques were introduced to incorporate the human factor into planning processes (World Bank, 1980). Many agencies adopted the Logical Framework to accommodate more rigorous evaluation techniques that included the intended beneficiaries as well as the identification of "causal linkages in the project environment" (Binnendijk, 1990).

In the evaluation of individual development projects, however, a dualism often still exists between what Casley and Kumar (1987) term "physical delivery projects" (including building and maintaining infrastructure and operating plants) and "people centered projects"—with the latter perceived as "more difficult to manage because of less tangible goals and less precisely specified means of attaining these goals" (1987). Infrastructure ("hard") sectors are often distinguished from social ("soft" or peopled) sectors. As development paradigms shift once again in the 1990s to include with greater rigor such concepts as effectiveness and sustainability, this dualism between peopled and nonpeopled projects is increasingly recognized as unhelpful.

Conceptual Frameworks for Gender Impact Evaluation

Why is a concern for gender important? Is it because development disadvantages women, because development needs women, or because development can empower women? Gender concerns are integrated into development initiatives to serve a wide range of goals. Since these initiatives are evaluated against their original goals, these goals have important implications for evaluating gender impacts and for choosing indicators to be used for measurement.

From Women in Development to Gender and Development. Whether or not the "gendering" of impact evaluation procedures calls for the development of a tailor-made methodology depends on the goal of the evaluation and on the type of constraints that affect project and program implementation. For example, is the evaluation to measure the impact on women, or the changes that have taken place in the gendered nature of society? Are the constraints on implementation technical and the consequence of inappropriate procedures, or are they political and cultural? Are they best overcome by augmenting or by changing procedures? Impact evaluation must be discussed within the conceptual framework for integrating women in the development process, which has been changing during the past decade.

Recognition of women's role in the development process is not new. However, just as in the past decades paradigms for economic development have shifted, so too views about women's roles in the development process have undergone fundamental changes as theoreticians and practitioners have reassessed women's contribution to development. The most important consequence of the fundamental paradigm shift that has taken place from Women in Development (WID) to Gender and Development (GAD) is that women are no longer treated as a special interest group but as an integral part of any development strategy that places women and men within their sociocultural and political context.

WID recognizes that women are active, if often unacknowledged, participants in the development process, providing a critical contribution to economic growth. This approach argues that, as an untapped resource, women must be brought into the development process. GAD, recognizing the limitations of focusing on women in isolation, highlights the need to look at women in society, at the social relations between men and women, and at the way in which unequal relations between these categories have been socially constructed (Moser, 1993).

Gender Roles and Gender Needs. Awareness of gender as an integral part of all development work has not automatically affected the procedures, tools, and techniques of development practice, but two key planning concepts—gender roles and gender needs—have proved particularly useful at the policy, program, and project levels.

In most poor households, men have the primary productive role. Women are responsible for reproductive work—the childbearing and rearing required to guarantee the biological and social reproduction of the labor force—but they also have a productive role as well as a community managing role. At the community level, men more generally are involved in community politics. The most important planning implication is that women, unlike men, are severely constrained by the need to balance three roles, with value placed only on their roles as paid laborers.

Because men and women have different roles and responsibilities within the household and different control over resources, they also often have different needs. The second key concept is the distinction between practical and strategic gender needs. *Practical gender needs* are the needs that women identify within their socially accepted roles in society. These perceived needs do not challenge the gender divisions of labor or women's position in society. They are identified within a specific context and include inadequacies in living conditions such as access to water, health care, and employment. *Strategic gender needs* are the needs women identify as arising from their subordinate position to men in their society. Meeting these needs helps women to achieve greater equality by changing their position in society. The strategic needs vary according to the context but relate to gender divisions of labor, political power, and the control of resources.

Linked to the shift from WID to GAD, changes have occurred in policy approaches to women in developing countries. Since the 1950s, shifts from "welfare" to "equity" to "anti-poverty," as categorized by Buvinic (1983), to two further approaches, which I have categorized as "efficiency" and "empowerment" (Moser 1989), have mirrored general trends in Third World development policies: from the modernization policies of accelerated growth, through redistributive strategies to meet basic needs, to the more recent compensatory measures associated with structural adjustment policies. Each of these policy approaches differs in terms of the roles recognized, the practical or strategic needs it meets, and the extent to which it incorporates participatory planning procedures (see Moser 1989, 1993).

Objectives of Gender Impact Evaluation: Implementation or Development Impact?

Development initiatives of any kind are difficult to evaluate when their objectives are unclear. Unclear objectives often cause difficulties in the assessment of gender impacts. For example, "to improve the status of women" is a classic example of a complex goal, with globally relevant composite indicators that are difficult to identify; "to bring women into development" is vague; and "to alleviate poverty and empower" is ambiguous (whether unintentionally or, as is more often the case, intentionally to conceal conflicting objectives between different actors involved).

To measure the achievement of goals, two sets of indicators are needed: first, indicators that monitor and evaluate the implementation of procedures, and second, indicators that assess or measure the impact of interventions on the situation of women (Moser, 1993). Much of the literature on gender indicators does not distinguish adequately between these types of indicators or consider the various interconnections between them (Beck, 1994).

The World Bank has identified key performance indicators as critical variables that can be used to measure implementation progress and development impact. This distinction is useful for gender impact evaluation. Table 7.1 shows the different objectives and indicators for both implementation and impact evaluation.

Evaluating Implementation. Given the widespread reluctance to introduce a gender perspective into development work, most agencies focus first on operationalizing such a perspective within their planning procedures.

Table 7.1. Evaluation of Gender Implementation and Impact

Types of Gendered Evaluation	Objectives	Indicators
Implementation evaluation	To evaluate implementation of operational procedures to institutionalize gender concern in agency and its planning procedures	Implementation indicators (see Table 7.2)
Impact evaluation	To evaluate the differential development impact on men and women	Effectiveness indicators of: Inputs Outputs Outcomes Impact

Table 7.2. Planning Procedures to Operationalize WID

General Procedures	Purposes	Type of Country-Specific Procedure
1. WID mandate or policy	To define and legitimize WID policy	Parliament legislation Ministerial directive Internal guidelines Operational objectives
2. Plan of action gies and procedures	To provide WID operational strate- WID strategy paper	Detailed plan of action General action programs
3. WID-specific sector guidelines	To provide sector-specific WID guidelines	Sector-level WID checklists WID sector papers WID manuals
4. Integrated WID criteria in sector guidelines	To integrate WID criteria into general sector guidelines	Sector guidelines WID office procedures
5. Country-level WID guidelines	To integrate WID criteria into general sector guidelines	Country-specific WID plans Country plan of action Country development strategy statement Country program/reports Country assessment WID papers
6. WID project guidelines	To integrate WID into the project cycle	WID project cycle manual WID project checklist Project identification document Project paper Checklist for participation of WID projects
7. Monitoring procedures	To monitor implementation of WID plan of action	Progress reports Built-in monitoring procedures Reporting to congress

Source: Moser, 1993, p. 145.

Table 7.2 identifies the goals of seven different planning procedures to operationalize a WID perspective (Moser, 1993). (Because objectives are important in determining the rationale for introducing gender, the development of a clearly articulated policy, followed by a plan of action or strategy paper, is generally the starting point. Performance indicators then relate to the completion and endorsement of such procedures by the agency.)

A second important area is the development project cycle. Detailed interventions to introduce gender-consciousness at each stage of the cycle include terms of reference for staff and consultants, training, and guidelines on the composition of mission teams (Table 7.3). For each of these interventions quantitative indicators can be developed.

To date, most development agencies have given priority to evaluating implementation procedures rather than impact and have institutionalized the use of indicators for this purpose. The U.S. Agency for International Development (1992), for example, stresses:

Operational requirements to establish the systems and procedures necessary for institutionalizing WID

Design and reporting procedures that reflect and address gender analysis and constraints

Agency staff awareness, to help institutionalize gender awareness

Women's participation in participants' training programs.

Britain's Overseas Development Administration (ODA) concentrates on expenditure commitments, on the number of women within ODA and from developing countries in ODA-provided training, and on recommendations on how to make the agency and the project cycle gender-sensitive (Oversees Development Administration, 1993).

A recent assessment of the OECD Development Assistance Committee's policies and programs for WID, undertaken for the 1995 Fourth United Nations Conference on Women, exemplifies the use of different evaluation indicators in its three theme studies (Organization for Economic Cooperation and Development, 1994). The first study, on "the integration of gender concerns in the work of DAC," assesses *documentation* on policy by identifying implementation indicators such as policy statements and principles, annual and aid reviews, statistical reporting, and work on sector reviews. The second study, on "the policies and organizational measures on WID adopted by DAC country members," uses implementation indicators to assess the *adoption* of WID policies and measures.

Evaluating Impact. The complexity of evaluating development impacts from a gender perspective is widely recognized. Less progress has been made here than in evaluating implementation. Many agencies are only now embarking on evaluating project effectiveness—and many so-called "gendered" projects are not yet at the evaluation stage. Even so, distinct stages in the development of gender impact evaluation can be identified.

Table 7.3. Checklist of Current Interventions to Gender the Project Cycle

Stage	Important Interventions
1. Identification	Policy direction Identification of WID policy approach (WID/GAD policy matrix) Targeted or mainstream intervention
2. Preparation (a) definition of target group (b) identification of gender objectives	Gender diagnosis Gender roles identification Gender-needs assessment
3. Design (a) personnel (b) socioeconomic feasibility studies	Staff gender training Gendered terms of reference for staff and consultants Mechanisms to ensure women and gender-aware organizations are included in planning process Gender-needs assessment Gender-disaggregated data over allocation and control of resources
4. Appraisal (a) mission personnel (b) appraisal studies	Gendered terms of reference for consultants Inclusion of gender expectations Gender staff training Gendered cost-benefit analysis to include women's "invisible work" Inclusion of women in staff gender training
5. Ratification	Entry points for dialogue Staff training on gender-awareness of issues
6. Implementation (a) agency and staff (b) target population	Staff gender planning training Gendered terms of reference for staff Gendered composition of agency Clarification of women's role in participatory projects
7. Monitoring/evaluation	Gendered terms of reference for consultants Staff gender training Team composition

Source: Moser, 1993, p. 157.

Grafting Women onto Impact Evaluation: Gender-Disaggregated Data. "What is not counted is usually not noticed" (Galbraith, cited in Overholt, Anderson, Cloud, and Austin, 1985). The first crucial stage in evaluating gender impacts is to make women "visible" through the introduction of gender-disaggregated data. The goal is twofold: to quantify the full extent of women's participation in economic and social life (the economic justification for investing in women) and to demonstrate women's true status in terms of income, health, and education as well as legal and other human rights (the equity justification for gender concerns).

Twenty-five years after Boserup's formative work (Boserup, 1970), progress is still very slow, despite an extensive literature showing the underestimation of the economic and social value of women's domestic and nonmarket production. The OECD review noted that although the proportion of the sample supplying sex-disaggregated data had risen from 30 percent in 1989 to 45 percent in 1993, several donors reviewing their own evaluations were puzzled by the lack of gender-disaggregated data, given the length of time over which their WID policies and directives had been in place (OECD, 1994).

Disaggregating data by gender is critical to make women visible, but it does not ensure that project objectives are gendered; it only uncovers the tip of the iceberg (Evans, 1992). Complex problems exist. These are not only definitional—relating to such concepts as household and headship—but also ideological or judgmental—relating to the different values accorded to male and female economic, informal, and nonmarket activities (Waring, 1988; Beneria, 1992)—and methodological—relating to problems in the evaluation of intrahousehold resource allocation and to the assumption that methods and techniques to elicit data work equally well for men and women (Evans, 1992).

Mainstreaming Gender into Impact Evaluation: Gender Analysis and Consultation Procedures. During the past five years, agencies have increasingly sought to mainstream a concern for gender into development initiatives. This has required the inclusion of additional methodological frameworks, many of them effectively introduced through staff training. Three operational procedures are particularly important in developing indicators for use in evaluating impacts:

1. A comprehensive gender analysis—an adequate database on what women do and why (Overholt, Anderson, Cloud, and Austin, 1985); identification of contextually specific problems of development for men and women; and a description of the relationships between these problems, with a cause and effect hierarchy established (Moser, 1993). Tools and techniques based on either the Harvard gender analysis or the gender planning methodology or a combination of the two (Canadian Council, 1989) enhance the capacity of agencies to identify gender objectives (Netherlands Ministry of Foreign Affairs, 1994; U.S. Agency for International Development, 1988).

2. The participation of women and gender-sensitive local organizations throughout the planning process. This is now recognized as essential to ensure that the needs and interests of women as much as men are identified and met, and that women are active participants rather than passive beneficiaries in projects (Moser, 1993).

3. Institutional analysis to identify the extent to which institutions are capable of analyzing gender differences and applying gender-specific approaches. The level of emancipation within the organization "can be measured by parameters like the ratio of male to female staff; the levels and specific occupations in which men and women predominate; facilities and support systems provided for women staff" (Netherlands Ministry of Foreign Affairs, 1994).

Gender Impact Indicators. The early stage of development of appropriate indicators for measuring gender impact is made plain in the third of the DAC studies referred to above, on "WID as a cross-cutting issue in development and evaluation" (Organization for Economic Cooperation and Development, 1994). This study analyzed 1,315 evaluation reports from sixteen countries covering eight major sectors, focusing on aid in the form of projects and on project evaluations (Table 7.4). It considered direct or indirect effects on target groups, using a combination of implementation and impact indicators, but none of these indicators is able to measure the impact of interventions on the lives of women beneficiaries.

The indicators that are appropriate vary depending on the definition of project goals and benefits. For example, are the indicators meant to measure changes in women's lives brought about by a specific activity (United Nations, 1984), or to measure gender-related changes in society over time (Beck, 1994)? How are such impact changes measured?

Gender-needs assessment does not itself provide specific indicators but is a useful tool for grouping indicators relating to different aspects of women's subordination (Beck, 1994). Although impacts relating to practical gender needs may be measured quantitatively, impacts relating to strategic gender needs are less receptive to physical or economic interventions and call for indicators capable of measuring changing processes (Moser, 1993). Beck, for instance, typologizes effectiveness indicators as economic (focusing on control of assets, wage, parity, access to credit); social and cultural (focusing on nutrition, access to and parity in health and education, and social standing) and political (focusing on participation, power, and rights).

Table 7.4. Indicators in a WID Evaluation Study

Type of Indicator	Indicator
Implementation	WID/GAD issues in the evaluation terms of reference Women in evaluation teams WID/GAD specialists in the evaluation teams
Impact	A "full," "partial," or "not at all" discussion of gender issues Gender-disaggregated data Projects or programs that allocated all or part of the budget to WID/GAD

In theory, the framework adopted by many development assistance agencies requires four interrelated indicators to measure inputs, outputs, effect, and impact. In practice, many evaluations simply refer to impact indicators generically without differentiating further. Carvalho and White (1994), in their recent work on poverty reduction indicators, shift the focus away from evaluation itself to emphasize the importance of monitoring. In developing gender impact indicators a three-fold distinction can be made between input, output, and impact indicators. Most widespread to date are input indicators that measure the number of women as intended beneficiaries, identified through gender-disaggregated data on intended project beneficiaries. A recent overview of gender issues in the World Bank's lending, for instance, evaluates 615 projects in terms of their "WID/gender-related actions," using a rating system that covers intended gender-related actions at project appraisal but does not reflect what was achieved (Murphy, 1995). ODA's Policy Information Marker System WID Marker goes beyond the identification of women as beneficiaries to measure women as intended project participants.

Although gender-differentiated output indicators have long been used in social sectors such as health, education, and family planning, initiatives to develop performance indicators focusing on the clients/users of physical infrastructure provide important opportunities for identifying critical entry points for gender indicators. Recent work by the Swedish International Development Agency on water resource management illustrates indicators to measure gender-differentiated project output, using tools such as gender role identification, intra-household resource allocations, and gender-needs assessments (Swedish International Development Agency, 1994).

Gender indicators can be introduced through training. At a recent workshop in Indonesia to discuss the findings of a World Bank impact evaluation of the bank's support for Indonesia's Transmigration Program, gender role identification was used as a tool to demonstrate the differential impact of the program on men and women and on their gender roles. Although the Transmigration Program had little direct impact on women in their reproductive role, it significantly affected them in their productive role.

If project objectives are to meet strategic gender needs, then impact indicators need to measure gender-related changes in society. Most common are composite indicators that measure changes in education, health, nutrition, and income as proxy measures of women's status and gender equity. The Human Development Index of the United Nations Development Programme, with its gender index factored in, is currently the most comprehensive global index (United Nations, 1991).

With the shift from equity to empowerment, however, the emphasis has moved from static measurements of status to indicators that measure processes. What Sen (1990) calls "the process of politicization" is an important indicator of changing gender perceptions. Here the role that collective action plays in changing women's self-perception of status and power is critical in shifting intra-household gender-based asymmetries in access to welfare and productive resources (Moser, 1993).

Bennett, in her work on group-based financial services, defines empowerment as an increase in an individual's or group's self-confidence and capability to take action, and identifies the major settings within which empowerment may occur as the private sphere of the household, and the public spheres of the self-help group, the community, and beyond (Bennett, n.d.). Schuler and Hashemi (1994) describe a particularly interesting composite empowerment indicator developed in a comparative impact evaluation of Grameen Bank and Bangladesh Rural Academy of Comilla rural credit programs.

Can Indicators Measure Transformative Processes? Qualitative Evaluation Techniques and Triangulation

"In no area are there greater problems about measuring quality of life than in the area of women's lives and capabilities" (Nussbaum and Sen 1993). Recognizing the difficulties of quantifying intricate changes in gender relations, analysts have adopted a range of qualitative approaches, including participatory anthropological techniques. Some analysts have used triangulation, combining different quantitative and qualitative techniques and their associated indicators. Particularly relevant to the development of triangulated techniques are the participatory nonhierarchical procedures associated with women's organizations and self-help groups, developed by women themselves to identify their own needs. Alongside these procedures have developed institutionalized phenomenological approaches that seek to understand social reality from the perspective of groups and individuals. Best known is participatory rural appraisal (PRA), originally developed to recognize the indigenous technical knowledge of poor farmers and now extended to other participatory assessment and evaluation methods (Chambers, 1994). Gender-disaggregated participatory appraisal techniques such as participatory mapping; transect, wealth, or wellbeing ranking; and matrix ranking are used to determine not only the different needs and interests of men and women but also the differences between women of different classes and income groups.[1]

An ongoing four-city research project by the World Bank on Urban Poverty and Social Policy in the Context of Adjustment illustrates some of the complexities of a triangulated methodology. The research examines the wider development impact of macroeconomic policy from a gender perspective—the strategies adopted by poor urban households, and individual men and women within them, to reduce vulnerability and prevent further impoverishment during a period of macroeconomic recession and reform (Ravallion, 1992). In all four cities it combines three identical tools: a random sample survey to provide longitudinal trend data on a community, a smaller qualitative subsample used to explore intra-household decision-making processes, and a qualitative community-level survey providing information on the wider social context. The challenge for such triangulated approaches to evaluation is a broader recognition that the qualitative documentation of change processes goes beyond anecdotal, apt illustration, and that it complements quantitative impact indicators.

Conclusion

In highlighting the importance of evaluating gender impacts, this chapter has sought to document how different objectives have resulted in diverse methodological techniques. Although appropriate indicators of wider development impact are still at an exploratory stage, many of the more innovative participatory techniques that challenge the supremacy of quantitative indicators have much to contribute to current mainstream debates about changing evaluation paradigms.

References

Beck, T. "Literature Review of Social Gender Indicators." Paper prepared for Canadian International Development Agency (mimeo), 1994.

Beneria, L. "Accounting for Women's Work: The Progress of Two Decades." *World Development*, 1992, *20* (11), 1547–60.

Bennett, L. "Participation and Group-Based Financial Services Study, Guidelines for Data Analysis and Collection." Sociological Instruments, n.d. (Mimeographed)

Binnendijk, A. "Donor Agency Experience with the Monitoring and Evaluation of Development Projects." In K. Finsterbusch, J. Ingersoil, and L. Llewellyn (eds.), *Methods for Social Analysis in Developing Countries*. Boulder, Colo.: Westview Press, 1990.

Boserup, E. *Women's Role in Economic Development*. New York: St. Martins Press, 1970.

Buvinic, M. "Women's Issues in Third World Poverty: A Policy Analysis." In M. Buvinic, M. Lycette, and W. McGreevey, *Women and Poverty in the Third World*. Baltimore, Md.: John Hopkins University Press, 1983.

Canadian Council for International Cooperation/Match International. *Two Halves Make a Whole: Balancing Gender Relations in Development*. Ottawa: Canadian Council for International Cooperation, 1991.

Carvalho, S., and White, H. *Indicators for Monitoring Poverty Reduction*. World Bank Discussion Paper no. 254. Washington, D.C.: World Bank, 1994.

Casley, D., and Kumar, K. *Project Monitoring and Evaluation in Agriculture*. Baltimore, Md.: John Hopkins University Press for the World Bank, 1987.

Cassen, R., and associates. *Does Aid Work? Report to an Intergovernmental Task Force*. Oxford, England: Clarendon Press, 1986.

Cernea, M. (ed.). *Putting People First: Sociological Variables in Rural Development*. New York: Oxford University Press for the World Bank, 1985.

Chambers, R. "The Origins and Practice of Participatory Rural Appraisal." *World Development*, 1994, *22* (2).

Evans, A. "Statistics." In L. Ostergaard (ed.), *Gender and Development: A Practical Guide*. London: Routledge, 1992.

Hicks, N., and Streeten, P. "Indicators of Development: The Search for a Basic Needs Yardstick." *World Development*, 1979, *7*.

Moser, C.O.N. "Gender Planning in the Third World: Meeting Practical and Strategic Gender Needs." *World Development*, 1989, *17*.

Moser, C.O.N. *Gender Planning and Development: Theory, Practice, and Training.* London and New York: Routledge, 1993.

Murphy, J. *Gender Issues in Bank Lending: An Overview.* Washington, D.C.: World Bank Operations Evaluation Department, 1995.

Netherlands Ministry of Foreign Affairs. "Gender Assessment Study: A Guide for Policy Staff." The Hague, Netherlands: Directorate General for International Development, Special Program Women and Development, 1994.

Nussbaum, M., and Sen, A. *The Quality of Life.* Oxford, England: Clarendon Press, 1993.

Organization for Economic Cooperation and Development (OECD), Development Assistance Committee. *Assessment of DAC Members' WID Policies and Programs: Overall Report.* Paris: OECD Development Assistance Committee, 1994.

Overholt, C., Anderson, M., Cloud, K., and Austin, J. *Gender Roles in Development Projects.* West Hartford, Conn.: Kumarian Press, 1984.

Overseas Development Administration. *Report on Progress in Implementing ODA's Policy on Women in Development.* London: Oversees Development Administration, Social Development Department, 1993.

Ravallion, M. *Poverty Comparisons: A Guide to Concepts and Methods.* Living Standards Measurement Study Working Paper 88. Washington, D.C.: World Bank, 1992.

Schuler, S., and Hashemi, S. "Credit Programs, Women's Empowerment, and Contraceptive Use in Rural Bangladesh." *Studies in Family Planning,* 1994, 25 (2).

Sen, A. "Gender and Cooperative Conflict." In I. Tinker, *Persistent Inequalities.* Oxford, England: Oxford University Press, 1990.

Swedish International Development Agency. "Towards a Framework for Including a Gender Perspective in Water Resource Management: Draft Framework," 1994. (Mimeographed)

United Nations. *Guiding Principles for the Design and Use of Monitoring and Evaluation in Rural Development Projects and Programs.* United Nations ACC Task Force on Rural Development: Panel on Monitoring and Evaluation. Rome, 1984.

United Nations. *Human Development Report.* New York: Oxford University Press, 1991.

U.S. Agency for International Development. *The Gender Information Framework: Gender Considerations in Design, Executive Summary.* Washington, D.C.: U.S. Agency for International Development, 1988.

U.S. Agency for International Development. "Working Paper on the Use and Analysis of Gender-Disaggregated Data and Indicators." Prepared by M. Malhotra, D. Caro, and V. Lambert. Washington, D.C.: U.S. Agency for International Development, 1992. (Mimeographed)

Waring, M. *If Women Counted.* San Francisco: Harper, 1988.

World Bank. *Human Factors in Project Work.* Staff Working Paper 397. Washington, D.C., 1980.

CAROLINE O. N. MOSER is a senior urban social policy specialist at the World Bank.

The author draws from the lessons of the ongoing Housing Indicators Program to provide a framework for developing better performance indicators and improving the development impact of housing policies and programs.

The Housing Indicators Program: A Model for Evaluation Research and Policy Analysis?

Stephen K. Mayo

The Housing Indicators Program—an ongoing collaboration between the World Bank and the United Nations Center for Human Settlements (UNCHS)—sets bold objectives: to alter fundamentally the way development institutions and governments think about the housing sector, to provide a framework and the information necessary to significantly improve the development impact of lending activities and policies for housing, and to contribute to the establishment of a new institutional relationship to produce long-lasting improvements in the formulation, implementation, and evaluation of the impacts of housing policy.

A basic tenet of this chapter is that evaluation needs tools and data not currently fully available to improve the performance of major economic sectors such as housing. Traditional World Bank evaluations have focused narrowly on the implementation performance of loans or on project impacts. Although useful in identifying operationally valuable lessons, such evaluations are not likely to be as useful in bringing about major improvements in the development impact of bank activities in the housing sector. Evaluation activities that focus on the overall performance of housing markets and the housing sector and on the sector's response to policies, institutions, and regulations are likely to be more useful.

Origins of the Housing Indicators Program

In the World Bank, the need for better performance indicators for measuring the development impact of lending for housing had been felt for several years.

In particular, by the mid 1980s it had become evident that despite the high success rates given to shelter projects by traditional World Bank evaluations, shelter projects were not having the development impacts that were considered either possible or desirable. For evaluation of impact at the sector level, additional tools and data were needed.

Disappointments with the traditional housing policies and programs of developing-country governments culminated in 1988 in a major United Nations policy document calling for sweeping changes in housing policies and programs typically applied in developing countries. The document, *A Global Shelter Strategy for the Year 2000*, called for a fundamental shift in governments' role in housing. Rather than attempting to provide housing directly, a policy that had usually failed, governments were urged to play an enabling role—one that would facilitate and support the activities of the private sector, both formal and informal, in housing development.

The Global Shelter Strategy created both the need and the opportunity for developing a framework for measuring housing sector performance, capturing aspects of performance and the policy and institutional regime by quantitative indicators, and developing tools to enable countries and development institutions to use information to improve housing sector performance. The Housing Indicators Program was formed with these needs and opportunities in mind.

Program Objectives and Activities

The overall objectives of the Housing Indicators Program are to develop conceptual, analytical, and institutional frameworks for managing the housing sector as a whole. More specifically, the program has four aims: (1) to provide a comprehensive conceptual and analytical framework for monitoring the performance of the housing sector; (2) to create a set of practical tools using quantitative, policy-sensitive indicators for measuring the performance of the housing sector and to test those tools in a broad range of countries; (3) to provide, through the results of an extensive survey, important new empirical information on the high stakes of policy making in the housing sector for societies and economies; and (4) to initiate new institutional frameworks that would be more appropriate for managing the housing sector and for formulating and implementing future housing policies in light of new research findings.

To date the program has developed, collected, and tested a broad range of such indicators in fifty-three countries; it has studied two housing sectors in detail (Hungary and the Philippines) with a view to addressing specific policy issues in those countries; it has analyzed the data obtained from the survey (particularly for insights into the connection between policies, institutions, regulations, and sector outcomes); it has developed protocols and examples for the application of housing indicator data to a variety of World Bank activities in housing; and it has developed a set of key indicators that can be collected regularly and disseminated globally.

The Conceptual Framework. Two simple concepts form the framework for the Housing Indicators Program. The first is that the performance of the housing sector is governed largely by market forces—by supply and demand—and that any comprehensive system of indicators must take into account not only housing outcomes but also their antecedents—factors that influence supply and demand. These factors necessarily include other background factors such as climate, topography, demography, and the level of economic development and policy variables relating to regulation, institutional arrangements, and enforcement.

The second is that the performance of the sector must be considered from the viewpoints of all of the key stakeholders—end users, suppliers and developers, financiers, and local and national governments. These viewpoints give rise to both a checklist of concerns and a rough understanding of their priority for each stakeholder group. It is important to note that neither of these concepts imposes anything as demanding as a fully specified econometric model of sectoral performance nor a theoretical welfare economic model of tradeoffs among outcomes by individual stakeholder groups or tradeoffs among outcomes desired by the different groups. Consistency, common sense, and comprehensiveness are perhaps the three most important attributes of a system of sectoral performance indicators.

The two concepts create a need for at least rudimentary models of how the housing sector works and of how key stakeholders view the benefits of its workings. In the Housing Indicators Program, a list of some 200 indicators of outcomes, suggested by housing research, was winnowed down to twenty-five "key" indicators, ten "alternate" indicators, and twenty "regulatory audit" indicators, constructed from responses to more than 100 questions on the policy, regulatory, and institutional framework likely to affect sectoral performance.

Data Collection. A comprehensive set of housing indicators was defined and tested in five cities in early 1991. Based on the results of the field test, a survey instrument, the Extensive Survey, was fielded from May to August 1991, with data collected by country-based consultants in fifty-two countries. Subsequently, data were collected on the fifty-third country, Russia. The selected countries span every continent, contain more than 80 percent of the world's population and more than 90 percent of its urban population, are at every level of economic development, and are representative of most major political systems and housing policy archetypes.

The survey focused on one major city in each country, in most cases the capital. The focus on cities rather than on countries was made for both practical and theoretical reasons. In many countries, data at the city level were thought to be more readily available than at the national level. Review of housing market data of developing countries had shown that although housing market parameters clearly differed from city to city, the structural similarities within countries were often greater than the differences. Because many of the most important policies affecting market behavior were determined at the local rather than the national level, it was important that data on outcomes and on the policies likely to affect them be observed at the same level.

Analysis of the Data. Although data were collected on a large number of housing sector indicators, early analysis focused on a minimal subset of ten key indicators, chosen for descriptive and diagnostic purposes. Taken together, the key indicators could be interpreted to give information about the health of the housing sector, to indicate whether or not the sector was functioning well from the standpoint of different stakeholders, and to identify the affliction, if there was one, and to suggest the likely cure. Indeed, the ten housing indicators are structurally no different from those used in medicine, where such indicators as temperature, blood pressure, and levels of blood chemicals are used to inform diagnosis, to suggest a course of treatment, and to monitor progress.

Each aspect of medical diagnosis, prescription, and monitoring represents the use of indicators, which a combination of medical research and accumulated evidence has shown to be relevant to critical aspects of physiological performance and capable of showing connections between cause and effect. The ten key housing indicators (defined in Table 8.1) have been similarly chosen— for their relevance to key stakeholder groups and for their ability to be related both hypothetically and empirically to policy and other variables.

In addition to the ten measures of housing outcomes, several other indicators were developed to characterize the policy regime. The most important of these is the Enabling Index, which measures the degree to which the policy and institutional environment is judged to facilitate the activities of housing sector stakeholders. The Enabling Index, which ranks cities on a scale of 0 to 100, is constructed by giving equal weight to each of six subindexes that characterize the policy regime: (1) housing finance, (2) the regulatory regime, (3) infrastructure adequacy, (4) industrial organization, (5) public sector involvement, and (6) property rights development. Each of the subindexes is made up of answers that were given in response to a comprehensive regulatory audit conducted as part of the Extensive Survey (see Angel and Mayo, forthcoming).

Various transformations of the Enabling Index and its components were tested for their usefulness in helping to explain place-to-place differences in housing outcomes, in each case within the context of multivariate models drawn from the literature on urban housing markets. From the early analysis, several general conclusions are emerging.

First, data from the Housing Indicators Program appear to be robust, capable of providing accurate pictures of housing sector performance in the different cities. Data reliability appears to be highly acceptable for most variables. For example, data from low-income countries appears not to be inherently more variable than data for high-income countries. Patterns of regularities in the data exist at all levels of economic development; such patterns appear to be broadly consistent with those found in other studies that have drawn together cross-country data on housing market outcomes.

Second, by using only the ten key indicators, evaluators can capture many, if not most, of the important dimensions of housing sector performance.

Table 8.1. Key Indicators of Housing Sector Performance

Type of Indicator	Indicator	Definition
Price	House price-to-income	Ratio of the median free-market price of a dwelling unit and the median annual household income
	Rent-to-income	Ratio of the median annual rent of a dwelling unit and the median annual household income of renters
Quantity	Housing production	Total number of housing units (in both formal and informal sectors) produced last year per 1,000 people
	Housing investment	Total investment in housing (in both formal and informal sectors in the urban area) as a percentage of gross city product
	Floor area per person	Median usable living space per person (in square meters)
Quality	Permanent structures	Percentage of housing units in structures built of permanent material
	Unauthorized housing	Percentage of the total housing stock in the urban area that is not in compliance with current regulations
Demand side	Housing credit portfolio	Ratio of total mortgage loans to all outstanding loans in both commercial and government financial institutions
Supply side	Land development multiplier	Average ratio between the median land price of a developed plot at the urban fringe in a typical subdivision and the median price of raw, undeveloped land in an area currently being developed
	Infrastructure expenditures per capita	Ratio of the total expenditures (operations, maintenance, and capital) by all levels of government on infrastructure services (roads, sewerage, drainage, water supply, electricity, and garbage collection) during the current year, and the urban population

Preliminary analyses that have simultaneously mapped outcomes on the ten key indicators have found patterns that strongly differentiate different types of countries. In some cases such patterns appear to represent merely the dichotomy of "healthy" or "well-functioning" markets versus "unhealthy" markets and in other cases to suggest a finer typology—one in which different policy pathologies are evidently influencing housing outcomes.

Third, place-to-place variation in housing market outcomes is considerable and can be shown to depend on referential indicators such as the level of economic development and demographic variables, and on policy differences. In many cases, the relationship between housing outcomes and income (whether reckoned in terms of gross national product per capita or household income) is statistically highly significant. Policy differences, as measured by the Enabling Index and its components, are usually, though not always, significantly related to housing sector outcomes. In some cases, enabling policies appear to work through the price system, changing and often lowering housing prices, which in turn influence both expenditures on housing and physical quantities. In other cases, the effects of enabling policies appear to transcend their evident price-influencing role.

Fourth, housing sector outcomes often appear to be more heavily influenced by policy and institutional differences than by short-run changes in the level of economic development. At any given level of economic development, significant place-to-place variations almost always are seen in housing outcomes, suggesting that the rate at which society's resources are translated into more and better housing is highly variable. In some cases, countries appear to attain housing virtually equivalent to that of countries with incomes five times as high. In most of these instances the differences in outcome appear to be the result of policy differences rather than factors such as culture, climate, or topography. Thus, poor quality housing often can be as much the result of housing policy as of poverty.

Several of these findings are elaborated on in the discussion on home price-to-income ratio (see Angel and Mayo, 1993, for more detail).

The house price-to-income ratio is the indicator that conveys the greatest amount of information on the overall performance of housing markets and is obviously a key measure of housing affordability. When housing prices are high relative to income, other things being equal, a smaller fraction of the population will be able to purchase housing. Equally important, this indicator provides important insights into several housing market dysfunctions, indicative of a variety of policy failures. An unusually high price-to-income ratio, for example, generally indicates that the housing supply system is restricted in its ability to satisfy effective demand for housing, a feature of many housing delivery systems in both market and centrally planned economies. In such cases, housing quality and space are often depressed below levels that are typical of countries with well-functioning and responsive housing delivery systems. An unusually low ratio may indicate widespread insecurity of tenure, a situation that reduces the willingness of the population to invest in housing and produces poorer housing than necessary.

Figure 8.1 illustrates the way the house price-to-income ratio varies across countries at different levels of GNP per capita. It shows the median reported value for five different average income levels, for a group of about ten countries for each income level, and displays the highest and lowest reported value of the indicator for each income grouping. Table 8.2 indicates variation across geographical regions. The preliminary results of the Extensive Survey are given below.

The mean reported house price-to-income ratio is 5.0 and ranges from a low of 0.9 to a high of 14.8. The reported median increases modestly with the level of economic development, consistent with the notion that increasing tenure security (a greater fraction of legal dwellings with tradeable property rights) increases the rate at which house rents are capitalized into values. Variation among regions is slightly more pronounced than with income, with the highest reported ratios in Europe, Middle East, North Africa, and South Asia and the lowest in sub-Saharan Africa, Latin America, and the Caribbean.

Reported ratios of house price-to-income are particularly high in countries with restricted private property rights and prominent public sector

Figure 8.1. House Price-to-Income Ratio and GNP Per Capita

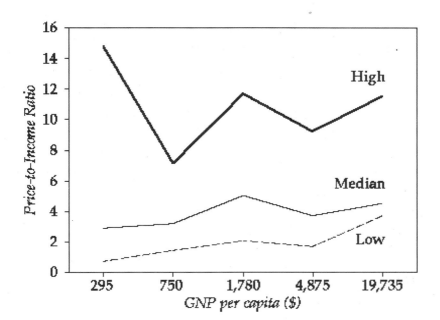

ownership of land and housing. The average value of the ratio for communist or former-communist countries (China, Czechoslovakia, Hungary, Poland, and Russia) is estimated to be about 9.2. Other countries with particularly high house price-to-income ratios are those with high construction costs and high land prices (for example, Algeria at 11.7, Hong Kong at 7.4, and Japan at 11.6), caused in part by tight regulatory environments that affect land use and housing construction, policies such as agricultural green belts, and complicated and time-consuming regulations. By contrast, the ratio is unusually low in countries with low and generally stagnant incomes and large fractions of unauthorized housing (for example, most countries of sub-Saharan Africa), suppressed demand resulting from heavy-handed intrusions by the government in housing markets (for example, South Africa at 1.7), and administratively controlled resale prices (for example, Singapore at 2.8).

On average, cities (countries) with relatively enabling housing policies have a ratio of house price-to-income of only 3.8., compared with 6.2 in cities with less enabling policies. In part because of the higher price of housing relative to incomes (and because of a higher incidence of rent controls) among those with less enabling policies, the rate of homeownership is correspondingly lower (43 percent versus 60 percent). In turn, because homeowners generally have higher levels of housing consumption than do renters, every measure of space-related housing consumption on which data were collected is higher among the cities with enabling policies (see Table 8.3).

Table 8.2. Variation in House Price-to-Income Ratio, by Region

Sub-Saharan Africa	2.21
South Asia	6.25
East Asia	4.15
Latin America and Caribbean	2.3
Europe, Middle East, and North Africa	6.59
Industrialized countries	4.70

Table 8.3. Measures of Space Consumption for Enablers and Non-Enablers

Indicator	Enablers	Non-enablers
Households	1.02	1.08
Persons per room	1.34	1.5
Floor area per person (M²)	16.2	11.1
Dwelling unit size (M²)	68.8	47.7

Note: M=Meter
Source: Unpublished data from the Housing Indicators Program, based on a sample of 53 cities, 26 of which are categorized as enablers and 27 as non-enablers. Data are for 1990.

Such contrasts are further heightened by comparisons between particular cities at similar levels of economic development. Urban households in Hong Kong and Athens, for example, have similar incomes but very different housing conditions and prices. In 1990, median dwellings in Hong Kong and Athens had 26 and 70 square meters of floor area and were valued at $112,000 and $54,000 respectively. Differences in costs are attributable to differences in land and construction costs, both of which are higher in Hong Kong than in Athens. These differences, in turn, reflect both demand and supply factors but particularly supply; in Hong Kong a combination of policies regarding tax, zoning, land use, and competition in the building industry have brought about a relatively unresponsive system of land and housing supply, as compared with Athens.

Similar differences are found among cities at every level of economic development, providing often striking evidence of how differently the fruits of economic growth are translated into measures of social well-being. Focusing attention on such differences in outcomes should encourage governments to explore successful new policies and strategies found in other countries.

Applications of Housing Indicators

Housing sector performance indicators can be used effectively by international development institutions at many stages of the project life cycle. Brief examples of some of the applications follow.

Establishing a framework for sector-level policy discussions between the lending institution and its borrowers. A recent World Bank Housing Policy Development Loan to the Republic of Korea was designed in part to address key structural problems in the Korean housing delivery system. The problems had resulted in extremely high housing prices, high economic rents associated with land development and housing construction, and badly targeted subsidies. In a jointly agreed on housing policy statement, which is incorporated into the loan document, the World Bank and the Korean government agreed that progress in reforming housing policies was to be measured using five key indicators related to the structural problems. (Four of the indicators are nearly identical to the key indicators used in the Housing Indicators Program.) Moreover, the loan was to be in direct support of broad sectoral objectives. The indicators would become part of a permanent system of sector monitoring, which would be used to gauge the efficacy not only of the recent World Bank– financed loan but also of any major policies affecting sector performance.

Establishing descriptive norms on key sectoral outcomes. Data from the Housing Indicators Program were used to establish descriptive norms for all the program's key and alternate indicators. Graphs such as the one presented in Figure 8.1 were produced for each indicator and along with relevant data were made available to operational staff for use in the field to help in determining whether housing markets were working normally.

Establishing a diagnostic framework for understanding when a sector is working well or badly, and why. In each of the countries where data and graphs were made available, staff were instructed on how to recognize policy pathologies based on findings of abnormal sectoral outcomes. In some cases, the application of the indicator framework suggests either that locally identified problems did not exist when proper data were brought to bear or that the problems were more symptomatic than structural.In the case of South Africa, for example, analysts in the country had identified a large housing deficit on the basis of shortfalls between recorded construction and known household growth. However, when indicators data were collected, the data revealed no housing deficit. Unrecorded informal construction had been going on at approximately the same rate as new households were being formed; nearly all persons were in fact housed. The indicators in part identified the real problems, most of which had stemmed from the pervasive influence of apartheid policies. The problems identified included grossly distorted housing locations (indicated in part by long journeys to work), low effective demand for housing (indicated by ratios of rent-to-income and house price-to-income), poor quality housing, and low investment (indicated by the ratio of housing investment to GDP), which was a consequence of low effective demand.

Identifying key areas for policy reform. In Korea, Malaysia, and South Africa elements of the policy pathology were identified using housing indicators of both housing sector outcomes and policy-related variables. In each of these countries, for example, the residential construction industry was highly concentrated, contributing to high construction costs. In the case of Korea and Malaysia, the unusual concentration was the product of a complicated and time-consuming regulatory regime that squeezed small housebuilders out of the market, leaving only large companies (which are far less responsive to demand shifts than small companies) to compete. In the case of South Africa, the concentration was a product of the apartheid system, which restricted commercial activities among nonwhites, and a general pattern of cartelization within South African industries. Although in each country some form of anti-monopoly policy reform appears necessary and might be included in a package of reforms, the underlying cause of housing concentration is one of inappropriate regulation. This problem has been identified as a key area for reform.

Identifying best practices to serve as models for intervention. Until recently few reliable examples of "best practices" were available to guide urban development staff of developing countries in designing better housing policies and programs. But performance indicator data, such as those from the Housing Indicators Program, permit evaluators to differentiate between real success stories and those clouded by exaggerated self-promotion and romanticized notions of success. At every level of economic development, countries show widely divergent housing outcomes. In general, the cities or countries with favorable housing outcomes given their levels of resources have either by design or accident discovered something that works in their policies, programs, institutions, or regulations.

What they discover may be less than perfect, but it is still able to produce compelling overall results worthy of consideration. For example, Bangkok is virtually a low-cost housing machine, the result of a dramatic change in less than a decade toward private-sector mass production of low- and moderate-income housing—in turn the result of a wide variety of enabling policies. Housing prices relative to incomes have fallen dramatically in a short period, and standards of space, quality, and tenure security have improved considerably. Yet Bangkok's traffic for its size is arguably the world's worst. Although common elements to the policies have produced both the good and bad conditions in Bangkok, the policies are not the same. No necessary tradeoff exists between good housing and bad transport. The data and framework from the Housing Indicators Program permit evaluators to examine how much success or failure is presented by the two faces of Bangkok's urban performance, to balance the two, and to begin to establish how good policies can be chosen without also incorporating the bad.

Facilitating research so that policies, institutions, and regulations influence key outcomes. A basic objective of the Housing Indicators Program is to establish links between housing sector policies and outcomes. Early analysis suggests that the program is well on the way to identifying and quantifying such links. Moreover, such indicators as the Enabling Index and its components appear promising in suggesting additional lines of research. Early and wide dissemination of program findings should stimulate analytical activity devoted to understanding the data, integrating them with other databases, and drawing implications for housing policies and sectoral outcomes.

Monitoring the effects of lending and policy and other reforms on outcomes. The Korean Housing Project used quantitative indicators, such as the house price-to-income ratio from the Housing Indicators Program framework, to measure the extent of problems in the housing sector. Also in Korea major policy reforms, such as the relaxation of residential zoning procedures, have been justified, in part, by indicator-based sector diagnostics.

Institutionalizing Housing Indicators

Ultimately, the test of any system of indicators, monitoring and evaluation, or policy analysis is whether or not it is actually used in improving decisions that have major and sustained impact on development outcomes. Whether or not such a system is used depends in part on its technical properties. Does it address the right issues? Does it give the right answers? Is it reliable? Is it cost-effective? Equally important, is it owned by the actors that have the power to make a substantial difference?

The Housing Indicators Program was designed with these requirements in mind. Thus it was designed as a global collaborative effort rather than as a narrowly focused case study carried out solely by the World Bank; it was designed as a tool-building exercise rather than as a program research project; and its design was made adaptable so that it could be of use to the many actors in the development process—international development institutions, national government agencies, local government agencies, and even the private sector.

The design is already showing results. Both UNCHS and the U.S. Agency for International Development (USAID) have adopted the program's framework and even the specific indicators in their own activities. UNCHS has established an indicators unit with responsibility for designing and implementing a global system for the collection of housing and urban development indicators. The starting point for this system is the ten key indicators described above, which UNCHS aims to collect universally within the next two years. The data collection effort is expected to be augmented by more extensive field surveys in selected countries, similar to the Extensive Survey of the Housing Indicators Program.

The regular collection of these key indicators will allow governments to begin monitoring the shelter sector on a regular basis, to detect whether progress is being made in attaining housing objectives, and to examine the effects of changes in shelter strategies on housing outcomes. The key indicators will form the core of a global monitoring strategy for the shelter sector, which can then be expanded and refined by individual governments to meet their specific needs and aspirations.

Toward these ends, the UNCHS Indicators Unit has responsibility not only for collecting data but also for providing training and technical assistance to governments in the design and use of policy-based housing and other urban indicators. Members of the unit have already organized and participated in several regional seminars on housing indicators and policy. Moreover, the framework created by the Housing Indicators Program has been endorsed by the preparatory committee of the upcoming international conference, the City Summit (also called Habitat II, coming twenty years after Habitat I), as the framework for the national reports to be presented at the conference. USAID has formally incorporated the indicators approach within a system of project performance indicators and is providing support to several governments in establishing their policy-based indicators systems.

Moreover, it is hoped that housing indicators data will be added to data published in World Bank, United Nations Development Programme, and UNCHS annual reports. The regular inclusion of housing indicators in international reports will focus needed attention on the importance of the housing sector in national economies and will lend impetus to new housing research aimed at understanding the reasons for differences in housing outcomes among and within countries. It will enable countries to compare their housing sector performance with that of other countries, particularly with countries that have similar characteristics. Moreover, it will raise interest among governments in putting in place their own systems of indicators to guide and inform policy choices and to monitor the performance of the housing sector.

References

Angel, S., and Mayo, S. K. *Housing: Enabling Markets to Work*. World Bank Housing Policy Paper. Washington, D.C.: World Bank, 1993.

Angel, S., and Mayo, S. K. *The Enabling Index: Quantifying Enabling Strategies and Measuring Their Impact on Housing Sector Performance*. Urban Development Department, World Bank. Washington, D.C.: World Bank, forthcoming.

United Nations Center for Human Settlements (UNCHS). *A Global Shelter Strategy for the Year 2000*. Nairobi, Kenya: United Nations Center for Human Settlements.

STEPHEN K. MAYO *is principal economist in the Urban Development Division of the World Bank and (with Shlomo Angel) co-director of the Housing Indicators Program.*

PART THREE

The Participatory Dimension

Sociocultural settings are missing variables in most evaluations of development projects and policies. An impending renaissance in applied sociocultural studies will enhance evaluation research and improve prospects for sustainable development impacts.

Including Culture in Evaluation Research

Robert Klitgaard

Imagine three assignments. First, you are to assess the effects of new decentralized government structures on the quality of local governance. Second, you are to evaluate the reasons why some local communities seem to have experienced rapid economic and social development while others (with different ethnic characteristics) have languished. Third, you are to evaluate the success of alternative educational programs for an indigenous minority group. How would you proceed?

Your first concern would probably be to know how to measure success. What might be meant by the quality of local governance and how might it be gauged? In the case of the local communities, how are such problematic concepts of economic and social development to be understood and measured? For the educational programs, what does success mean and how might it be measured in practice?

Your next problem would be to devise a framework to incorporate a variety of intervening variables that might affect success. You would probably want to control for some economic variables. For example, you might suspect that decentralized government structures produce better governance in richer districts, that local communities with ample natural resources and surrounded by relatively affluent communities do better economically and socially, and that schools whose students come from relatively affluent families do better educationally. If your evaluation does not control correctly for these economic variables, your findings may be biased. What other variables would you include, how would they be measured, in what multivariate model?

This chapter argues that evaluators usually should try to take account of differences in sociocultural contexts. First, the appropriate choice of dependent variables and measures may depend on the sociocultural setting. Utility functions may differ locally. The techniques used to measure outcomes—such as ways of eliciting local knowledge and undertaking action research—may need to be attuned to different sociocultural contexts.

Second, the strength of program or policy effects may depend on aspects of the sociocultural context. Recent research demonstrates that taking culture into account can improve the evaluation of decentralized governance, economic and social development, and educational interventions.

Sociocultural Setting as Symbolic Soil

Culture is a notoriously vague and problematic term. This chapter uses the related concept of sociocultural setting to refer to shared meanings, customary institutions, and something akin to a collective personality. Sociocultural settings cannot be assumed to be homogeneous, monolithic, or immutable, even locally. Rather they are multiple, overlapping, and subject to the forces of history and ecology. A metaphor of Putnam's (1993) is useful: local sociocultural conditions are the *symbolic soil* in which development takes place. Policies and projects may work better or worse, depending in part on the soil conditions; if we understood the soil conditions better, we might choose a different kind of policy or project. (Let us interpret the *we* broadly to include not only policy makers and evaluators but also peoples throughout the world as we strive in various ways to accelerate, modify, and avoid "development" of various kinds.) An important task for evaluation, indeed for applied social science, is to help in the understanding of these "policies by culture" interactions. Let us return to our three evaluative problems.

Decentralized Governance. Putnam and his team (1993) studied Italy's experience in the 1970s with the decentralization of many government functions to the provinces. After controlling for differing economic conditions across the provinces, the researchers discovered that the best predictor of good governance was the province's civic culture. This could be measured in a variety of ways, including by attitudes and voting behavior, but also by the density of civic associations. Historical data on those associations permitted a longitudinal analysis, which showed that causation ran from civic culture to economic growth to effective local government. Putnam concluded that government works best in sociocultural settings characterized by many horizontal civic associations—as opposed to vertical associations of the patron-client variety.

In evaluative terms, this means that an estimate of the effects of decentralization will be biased unless the evaluation takes into account the degree of civic participation in each province. The quality of governance (G) is a function not only of the policy change of decentralization (Decent) but also of the sociocultural setting (SCS), local economic conditions (Econ), and perhaps other variables, as in the schematic equation:

(1) $G = G(Decent, SCS, Econ, \ldots)$

Putnam's current research addresses the practical implications. Can governmental reforms somehow be tailored to local sociocultural settings? Can civic participation be enhanced, and at what costs?

Economic and Social Development Across Native American Tribes. Cornell and Kalt (for example, 1991, 1992) have evaluated the differences in economic and social development among Native American tribes. Some tribal economies have been growing at 8 percent a year, whereas others have been declining at 5 percent a year. Other outcome measures, such as unemployment rates, years of education, and alcoholism rates, also vary markedly across tribes.

These are the success measures in their study. What might be the intervening variables? Such influences as natural resources and economic conditions in areas adjacent to the tribes accounted for little of the variation across tribes.

Cornell (a sociologist) and Kalt (an economist) combined fieldwork with careful appraisal of previous ethnographic research. They asked people to tell them stories. Which people? Present and former heads of tribal governments, development officers, investors, and so forth. What stories? Stories about turning points in tribal life, about successful and unsuccessful entrepreneurs, and about resource use and investment. At the same time, the researchers gathered data about institutions and attitudes. In particular, they studied the separation of powers in tribal governance, the boundaries (social and geographical) perceived within the tribe and between the tribe and neighboring entities, and authority structures in the tribe and in the smaller groupings within it. They also examined aspects of collective identity (for example, to which groups did people say they belonged?).

Their statistical work showed that, after controlling for other variables, the match between current and traditional institutions influences economic and social development. For successful development, an institution has to be efficacious, and it has to fit within cultural preferences and normative orders. Also important is the match between the types of projects undertaken and certain cultural norms (for example, the tolerance for hierarchy).

Which sociocultural variables prove most important? Cornell (in Klitgaard, 1993) cites several: mechanisms for dispute resolution (current and traditional); tolerance of outsiders; tolerance of hierarchy (that is, willingness to obey orders); attitudes toward resources; the legitimate locus of authority, including the separation of powers; and organizational boundaries (that is, where does a person's allegiance lie?).

Better Education for Indigenous Minorities. A third example tailors policy to the sociocultural context. The Kamehameha Elementary Education Program (KEEP) in Hawaii designed culturally appropriate pedagogies to avoid "relatively narrow-range mismatches or incompatibilities between the natal culture of the children and the culture of the school at points that are critical for school success" (Vogt, Jordan, and Tharp, 1987, p. 286).

Hawaiian students often are viewed by school personnel as unmotivated and hard to manage. KEEP carried out a series of studies and interventions in the hope that correcting motivational problems would enable at-risk Hawaiian students to master their school work. At first it provided positive reinforcement in a phonics-oriented reading system, using criterion-referenced objectives and tests and frequent monitoring, with feedback to students and teachers. But scores on standardized tests—the authors' principal measure of success—did not rise.

Next, KEEP attempted to understand the children's Hawaiian culture and adapt classroom practices to it. Studies suggested that teacher-controlled student participation, in which each child took a turn reading, conflicted with the more interactive approach of traditional storytelling (Watson-Gegeo and Boggs, 1977; Au and Jordan, 1981). Classroom recitations reminded students of scoldings at home. KEEP therefore experimented with several changes.

First, instruction focused on meaning and comprehension with the teacher responding to children's talk, rather than concentrating on decontextualized skills drills. The new instructional focus seemed to open the door for the students to contribute in a speech style that was linguistically familiar to them. Second, the new system allowed more helping and sharing in the classroom. Third, praise was directed less at individuals than at groups of students. Ethnographic work indicated that indirect praise and praise to a group were more effective than direct praise that spotlighted one child.

These interventions worked. The test scores of Hawaiian students rose. Interestingly, when designers tried to replicate their experience at a Navajo reservation, they soon discovered differences. For example, the combination of love and toughness that had proved useful with Hawaiian children proved confrontational with Navajo children. Although Vogt and others (1987) argue that ethnographic research is necessary to tailor education to different cultural groups, they offer no model or theory to guide the development of culturally appropriate pedagogies.

Sociocultural Issues in Development Evaluations

These three examples show that sociocultural settings can interact powerfully with policy choices. For an evaluator, these interactions have three implications. First, evaluation of a program's effects may be biased unless sociocultural settings are correctly controlled for. Second, with sufficient knowledge the choice of programs might be tailored to the sociocultural setting. Third, local groups and communities might draw on this knowledge to change aspects of their sociocultural setting.

In international development, as in other policy domains, exhortations to take culture into account are plentiful but the know-how is scarce. This stark conclusion, illustrated below, is based on an analysis of the literature reported elsewhere (Klitgaard, 1991b).

Too Voluminous + Too Simplistic = No Impact. The German Agency for Technical Cooperation (GTZ) held a seminar in 1991 to address the continuing problems of communications and interaction between social science academics and development practitioners. Seminar organizers were seeking successful stories of interaction between social scientists and development practitioners (Steiner, 1991), but none was to be had: everywhere, seminar participants reported, the noneconomic social sciences were marginalized in development assistance.

Although attempts had been made to install checklists of sociocultural factors, the failures of such efforts, sometimes after fifteen years of experience, displayed some common features. For example, Germany's Federal Ministry for Economic Cooperation (BMZ) promulgated a list of sociocultural key factors in development cooperation to guide feasibility and impact assessment studies. The list, according to anthropologist Hans-Dieter Evers (1991), came under fire for several reasons, one being that it was not comprehensive enough. But in Evers's view BMZ's list was too broad, tended to cover all possible sociocultural variables, and spawned encyclopedic reports too bulky and difficult to digest. Consequently, the reports' sociocultural analyses served only as background information and proved ineffectual as recommendations for action.

Better Social Soundness Analyses = No Effect on Project Success. An assessment (Gow and others, 1989) of the oldest of these checklists, namely the guidelines for social soundness analysis in the U.S. Agency for International Development (USAID), produced similar results. The study examined a sample of fifty USAID projects (carried out from 1975 to 1981), using the following:

Measures of success: the project achieved few (1), some (2), or most (3) of its stated goals—no matter how ambitious the goals or how large the social costs and benefits that actually resulted.

A list of three subjective sociocultural characteristics: "sociocultural feasibility," defined by Gow and colleagues as "the compatibility of the project with the sociocultural environment in which it is to be introduced"; "spread effects," defined as "the likelihood that the new practices introduced among the initial target population will be diffused among other groups"; and "social consequences and benefit incidence," defined as "the social impact on distribution of benefits and burdens among different groups, both within the initial project and beyond" (1989, p. 24).

Simplistic measures of the quality of social analysis (on a 0 to 3 scale for each of the three issues): no mention of issue (0), brief mention but no analysis (1), intermediate level of analysis (2), full analysis of issue and some identified means of addressing it (3).

Using the study's appendixes, I performed some of the statistical analyses the study omitted. The results in Table 9.1 show no correlation between the quality of the social soundness analysis and the eventual success of the project.

Table 9.1. Statistical Analysis of a Sample of
Fifty USAID Projects, 1975–1981

Success = 1.87 + 0.11 (Quality of Overall SSA)
(0.16)
$R^2 = 0.01$, r = 0.10

Success = 1.87 + 0.085 (Quality of Feasibility Analysis)
(0.13)
$R^2 = 0.01$, r = 0.09

Success = 2.09 - 0.048 (Quality of Analysis of Spread)
(0.13)
$R^2 = 0.00$, r = 0.05

Success = 1.79 + 0.16 (Quality of Analysis of Consequences)
(0.12)
$R^2 = 0.03$, r = 0.19

S = 1.70 - 0.33 (Afr) + 0.16 (Asia) + 0.12 (Feas) - 0.11 (Spread) + 0.17 (Cons)
      (0.28)   (0.26)   (0.17)   (0.15)   (0.14)
$R^2 = 0.129$

Note: Standard errors are in parentheses. None of the coefficients is statistically significant at conventional levels. Means are: Success = 1.98, overall quality of SSA = 1.50, feasibility = 1.98, spread = 0.98, and consequences 1.55. SSA is social soundness analyses.
Source: Based on the author's reanalysis of data in Gow and others (1989).

In the same study, Gow and others also examined a small sample of twenty-seven projects carried out from 1982 to 1989, with the drawback that many of the evaluations of project success were midterm rather than final evaluations. The social soundness analyses were poorer in this sample than in the 1975–1981 sample (the mean was 1.13 on a scale of 0 to 3, compared with 1.50 in the earlier sample). The authors attributed the low overall scores to selective use of the social soundness analysis guidelines. Only two of the twenty-seven project designers followed all the guidelines.

"As with the first sample," the authors reported, without giving the correlations, "there is a direct association between feasibility and evaluation [that is, project success]" (p. 37). The relevant data, found in two separate parts of the appendixes, enabled this author to calculate a correlation of 0.09 for direct association in the 1975–1981 sample and a correlation of 0.12 for the 1982–1989 sample, neither of which is statistically significant. To put these numbers in perspective: among the fifty projects from 1975 to 1981, the study rated nine as having feasibility analyses of 3, the highest measure. The eventual success of these projects averaged 1.83 on a 1 to 3 scale. Only one project had a feasibility rating of 0; its eventual success was rated as 2. Eleven projects had feasibility ratings of 1. Their eventual success averaged 1.91.

Alleged Impact but No Model of Why or How. In a study of a non-random selection of fifty-seven World Bank–financed projects designed during the 1960s and early 1970s, Kottak (1991) estimated that "the average economic rates of return for projects that were socioculturally compatible and were based on an adequate understanding and analysis of social conditions were more than twice as high as those for socially incompatible and poorly analyzed projects" (pp. 434–435). Kottak's methodology was admittedly crude: for example, "projects were coded as incompatible only when the lack of social fit was substantial and obvious" (p. 435)—obvious to Kottak, subjectively, though evidently not to those designing the projects. He admits that the results should not be taken as "a hard, probability sample-based statistic, but as a trend indicator, significant for reflection" (pp. 437–438).

Regarding the sociocultural dimensions for study, Kottak lists such factors as participant incentives, human resources (specifically, the availability of manpower), land tenure, socioeconomic stratification, ethnicity, and women's roles. He does not define these operationally, nor does he suggest how the many factors might be simultaneously taken into account. He thus gives no helpful answer to the crucial question: how would knowing such variables change the choice of projects or designs?

Assessing the Importance of Cultural Factors

Why have policy-by-sociocultural-setting interactions been so elusive? One reason is that such interactions are very difficult to evaluate. The history of an analogous problem—the search for aptitude-by-treatment interactions in psychology—is instructive. For decades psychometricians have sought to validate an equation analogous to equation (1) in education. Is learning (L) a joint function of aptitudes (A) and pedagogical treatments (T), and perhaps of other personality variables (P) such as field-dependence, anxiety, and extroversion?

$$(2) \; L = g \, (A, \, T, \, P \, . \, . \, .)$$

Recent work has shown that the estimation of such statistical relationships is even more precarious than was previously thought (see, for example, Ackerman, Sternberg, and Glaser, 1989; Reuchlin, Lautrey, Marendaz, and Ohlmann, 1990; Snow, 1989). From the psychometric literature several conclusions can be drawn for assessing policy-by-sociocultural-setting interactions.

First, teasing out interaction effects turns out to be extremely complicated. Even if random assignment of policies across sociocultural settings were possible—which it is not, leading to unknown problems of endogeneity—estimating interaction effects is complicated by the many kinds of effects or combinations of effects (on the rate of change, the immediate or starting level, the asymptote or equilibrium toward which the development in question progresses) that may differ across sociocultural settings. The psychometric literature shows that within-group effects may cloud comparisons across groups. The assumptions of linearity or even of a multiplicative relationship (as in the inclusion of a P x SCS [sociocultural setting] term) may be inaccurate. Second, measurement errors make it difficult to discover interaction effects, as does the use of ordinal measures. As a result, statistical simulations may show interaction effects where none exists and mask them where they do exist. Third, various measures of the sociocultural setting may be highly correlated (this is what it means to say that culture is a pattern of variables, an ensemble, a total social fact). The evaluator therefore faces statistical problems of multicollinearity. Fourth, lags almost certainly exist. The lag structure will probably be different for different variables and will have to be modeled. Fifth, measuring the sociocultural setting is even more complicated than the usual psychometric specification, which assumes that aptitudes and personality variables are fixed. Sociocultural settings are themselves outcomes of economic and political conditions as well as policy choices, as shown by:

$$(3)\ SCS = f\ (\text{economy, governance, policies, projects}, \ldots)$$

Culture is subject to change. Some of these changes may be planned; many may not be. Some can be avoided, slowed, or speeded up; others cannot. Consequently, even if a detailed and well-specified longitudinal study were available, the results pertaining to a cohort from many years ago might not apply to the present.

For all these reasons, recent statistical research has shown that discovering interactions is much more complicated than was thought even fifteen years ago. Even with the best of theories and data, researchers will face tremendous difficulties in specifying culture-by-anything interactions over time—and thus in predicting such interactions.

With regard to policy-by-sociocultural-setting interactions, reality is harsher still. Anthropology and sociology have provided nothing like a general equilibrium model to estimate the effects of sociocultural settings at a point in time or their evolution over time. Valid and reliable sociocultural measures are meager and data scarce, making application of complicated models currently unrealistic.

A Renaissance in Applied Sociocultural Studies?

Nonetheless, I am optimistic about the prospects for incorporating sociocultural data in evaluation and, eventually, in the design of development policies, projects, and management techniques. In a variety of disciplines we are seeing exciting intellectual advances concerning sociocultural factors in economic and political development. In addition to the examples concerning Italian decentralization, Native American tribe development, and Hawaiian education, recent work includes: (1) successful testing of a new cultural theory to help explain attitudes toward risk, resource management, and strategies for overcoming poverty (for example, Thompson, Ellis, and Wildavsky, 1990; Dake, 1992; Wildavsky, 1994); (2) anthropological research demonstrating that minorities' self-definition plays a strong role in determining their academic success (Ogbu, 1992); (3) new studies of African success stories that emphasize the roles of indigenous institutions (Dia, 1994); (4) new cross-country empirical work demonstrating the close connection over time among cultural variables, economic growth, and political variables (Inglehart, forthcoming); (5) Sowell's (1994) documentation of the importance of cultural and ethnic factors in economic, social, and political development; (6) applications of market research techniques, in combination with anthropological data gathering, to problems of rural development (Epstein, 1988); and (7) the application of cross-cultural information in an anthropological data bank to a practical problem of development policy (Romanoff, Carter, and Lynam, 1991).

In addition, new empirical studies rigorously demonstrate the importance of corporate cultures to business performance (Kotter and Heskett, 1992). Some economists have been analyzing the emergence and importance of social norms and what might be called sociocultural institutions (for example, North, 1990; Schotter, 1981). With regard to Africa, a variety of recent contributions emphasize, if less scientifically, the importance of differences in the sociocultural settings (Ake, 1988; Bourgoin, 1984, Buijsrogge, 1989; Centre International des Civilisations Bantu, 1989; Dia, 1994, Etounga-Manguelle, 1990; Kabou, 1991; Klitgaard, 1991a; and Mazrui, 1990).

New Approaches to Evaluation: Becoming More Like Soil Scientists

In this convergence, I believe we are witnessing what might be called a renaissance of applied sociocultural studies. A decade hence, I predict we will have many more provocative studies of how sociocultural settings interact with policy choices, management techniques, pedagogies, and other development choices. This is a debatable proposition, and I would be the first to acknowledge the obstacles to more rigorous and more practical work. For one thing, academic identities are at stake. It can become a battle of disciplinary virtue to maintain, for example, that sociocultural differences are unimportant once economic factors are correctly understood, or that culture should not be conceptualized as a set of variables but should be considered a holistic *fait sociale totale*. These battles can themselves resemble intercultural conflict, full of stereotyping, turf protecting, and failures to communicate. Fear of misuse of cultural information and, as mentioned above, the statistical difficulty of modeling and estimating interaction effects, are other factors. These obstacles can be avoided. But to do so will involve shifting our perception of how applied sociocultural studies might contribute to the analysis of international development activities.

Returning to Putnam's analogy—culture is the *symbolic soil* in which development takes place. To carry out their practical work, soil scientists analyze soils, using partial and incomplete measures of soil differences. Their typologies and empirical results do not pretend to capture all factors characterizing a soil area. Good soil scientists listen carefully to what local farmers say about their land and farming practices. Beyond just describing differences in soil conditions, they study the interactions among soil types, crops, and soil treatments. They specify an equation like equation (1), but they also take into account the fact that soils can be changed as in equation (3). Soil scientists use their knowledge of soil-by-crop interactions to help farmers decide what crops to grow given local soil conditions and what soil treatments to undertake.

Can social scientists become more like soil scientists? Social scientists, too, might seek to provide partial but useful measures of local sociocultural conditions to help local people make better decisions. They, too, would recognize that local people know much more about their conditions and practices than the social scientist may ever know, that comparative and theoretical science can at best provide new insights for local people to consider.

What kinds of research does this perspective recommend? Researchers should try to discover what classifications of sociocultural "soil conditions" might prove useful for specific issues and in specific settings. Soil scientists often rely on experts from other disciplines—agronomists, chemists, economists, geographers—to help them assess local conditions. Applied sociocultural studies should be similarly eclectic. The appropriate disciplines may well vary depending on whether the issue is socioculturally appropriate rural health clinics, credit and savings programs, producers' cooperatives, school pedagogies, economic policies, and so forth.

Exploring the possibility of intentional cultural change is controversial. It is indeed a first-order question whether sociocultural knowledge, necessarily incomplete and imperfect, could be misused. Cultural change is more problematic than soil treatment. Nonetheless, the soil science metaphor provides a useful guideline: the scientist's comparative and theoretical perspectives may be able to supplement local knowledge about soil conditions and soil-by-crop interactions, but decisions about change should be left up to the locals themselves.

To push this agenda forward, more theoretical and empirical research is needed to determine why various aspects of culture matter, and how. New theoretical work suggests that trust and compliance are crucial to development. The research of Cornell and Kalt and of Putnam independently analyze how trust and compliance can be enhanced or inhibited by the sociocultural setting.

Although the recent empirical research is promising, little quantitative information is available about the measures used, such as their reliability, the cost of collecting data about them, and their validity for various predictive purposes. To remedy this situation, empirical investigations using different measures will be essential. Several valuable suggestions and research agendas emerge—for example, the "cultural audit" of Wildavsky (1994) and Cornell and Kalt's continued exploration of the "matches" between traditional institutions and modern structures of governance.

After collecting such decentralized sociocultural data, the task is to study their connections with local development outcomes, such as indicators of economic development, loan repayment rates, success of family planning programs, educational outcomes. The results might in turn suggest experiments to local people, perhaps abetted by external assistance, as they try to take their symbolic soil conditions into account.

References

Ackerman, P. L., Sternberg, R. J., and Glaser, R. (eds.). *Learning and Individual Differences: Advances in Theory and Research.* New York: W. H. Freeman, 1989.

Ake, C. "Building on the Indigenous." In P. Frühling (ed.), *Recovery in Africa: A Challenge for Development Cooperation in the 90s.* Stockholm: Swedish Ministry for Foreign Affairs, 1988.

Au, K. H., and Jordan, C. "Teaching Reading to Hawaiian Children: Finding a Culturally Appropriate Solution." In H. Trueba, C. P. Guthrie, and K. H. Au (eds.), *Culture in the Bilingual Classroom.* Rowley, Mass.: Newbury, 1981.

Bourgoin, H. *L'Afrique malade du management.* Paris: Editions Jean Picollec, 1984.

Buijsrogge, P. *Initiatives paysannes en Afrique de l'Ouest.* Paris: Editions L'Harmattan, 1989.

Centre International des Civilisations Bantu, Libreville, Gabon. *Facteurs culturels et projets de développement rural en Afrique centrale: Points de repère.* Paris: Editions L'Harmattan, 1989.

Cornell, S., and Kalt, J. *Where's the Glue?: Institutional Bases of American Indian Economic Development.* Cambridge, Mass.: Kennedy School of Government, 1991.

Cornell, S., and Kalt, J. *Reloading the Dice: Improving the Chances for Economic Development on American Indian Reservations.* Cambridge, Mass.: Kennedy School of Government, 1992.

Dake, K. "Myths of Nature: Culture and the Social Construction of Risk." *Journal of Social Issues,* 1992, *48* (4).

Dia, M. "Indigenous Management Practices: Lessons for Africa's Management in the '90s'." In I. Serageldin and J. Taboroff (eds.), *Culture and Development in Africa,* vol. 1. Washington, D.C.: World Bank, 1994.

Epstein, T. S. *A Manual for Culturally Adapted Market Research (CMR) in the Development Process.* Bexhill-on-Sea, U.K.: RWAL Publications, 1988.

Etounga-Manguelle, D. *L'Afrique: A-t-elle besoin d'un programme d'adjustement culturel?* Ivry-sur-Seine, France: Editions Nouvelles du Sud, 1990.

Evers, H. D. *Optimizing the Use of Social Science Know-How in Development Cooperation.* In M. Schönhuth (ed.), *The Socio-Cultural Dimension in Development: The Contribution of Sociologists and Social Anthropologists to the Work of Development Agencies.* Sonderpublikation der GTZ, no. 249. Eschborn, Germany: Deutsche Gesellschaft für Technische Zusammenarbeit, 1991.

Gow, D., and others. *Social Analysis for the Nineties: Case Studies and Proposed Guidelines.* Bethesda, Md.: Development Alternatives, Inc., 1989.

Inglehart, R. *Modernization and Postmodernization: Cultural, Economic, and Political Change in 43 Societies,* forthcoming.

Kabou, A. *Et si l'Afrique refusait le développement?* Paris: Editions L'Harmattan, 1991.

Klitgaard, R. "Adjusting to African Realities." *The Wilson Quarterly,* 1991a, *15* (1).

Klitgaard, R. *In Search of Culture.* Washington, D.C.: World Bank, Africa Technical Department, 1991b.

Klitgaard, R. (ed.) *Assessing Cultures.* IRIS Research Report no. 2. College Park: Center for Institutional Reform and the Informal Sector, University of Maryland, 1993.

Kottak, C. P. "When People Don't Come First: Some Sociological Lessons from Completed

Projects." In M. Cernea (ed.), *Putting People First: Sociological Variables in Rural Development*. (2nd ed.) New York: Oxford University Press, 1991.

Kotter, J. P., and Heskett, J. L. *Corporate Culture and Performance*. New York: Free Press, 1992.

Mazrui, A. M. *Cultural Forces in World Politics*. London: James Currey, 1990.

North, D. C. *Institutions, Institutional Change and Economic Performance*. Cambridge, England: Cambridge University Press, 1990.

Ogbu, J. *Cultural Models and Educational Strategies of Non-dominant Peoples*. New York: City College of New York, 1992.

Putnam, R. B., with Leonardi, R., and Nanetti, R. Y. *Making Democracy Work: Civic Traditions in Modern Italy*. Princeton, N.J.: Princeton University Press, 1993.

Reuchlin, M., Lautrey, J., Marendaz, C., and Ohlmann, T. (eds.). *Cognition: L'individuel et l'universel*. Paris: Presses Universitaires de France, 1990.

Romanoff, S., Carter, S., and Lynam, J. *Cassava Production and Processing in a Cross-Cultural Sample*. New Haven, Conn.: Human Relations Area Files, Dec. 1991.

Schotter, A. *The Economic Theory of Social Institutions*. Cambridge, England: Cambridge University Press, 1981.

Snow, R. E. "Cognitive-Conative Aptitude Interactions in Learning." In R. Kantor, P. L. Ackerman, and R. Cudeck (eds.), *Abilities, Motivation, and Methodology*. Hillsdale, N.J.: Erlbaum, 1989.

Sowell, T. *Race and Culture: A World View*. New York: Basic Books, 1994.

Steiner, A. "Foreword." In M. Schönhuth, ed., *The Socio-Cultural Dimension in Development: The Contribution of Sociologists and Social Anthropologists to the Work of Development Agencies*. Sonderpublikation der GTZ, no. 249. Eschborn, Germany: Deutsche Gesellschaft für Technische Zusammenarbeit, 1991.

Thompson, M., Ellis, R., and Wildavsky, A. *Cultural Theory*. Boulder, Colo.: Westview, 1990.

Vogt, L. A., Jordan, C., and Tharp, R. G. "Explaining School Failure, Producing School Success: Two Cases." *Anthropology and Education Quarterly*, 1987, *18* (4).

Watson-Gegeo, K. A., and Boggs, S. "From Verbal Play to Talk Story: The Role of Routines in Speech Events among Hawaiian Children." In C. Mitchell-Kernan and S. Ervin-Tripp (ed.), *Child Discourse*. New York: Academic Press, 1977.

Wildavsky, A. "How Cultural Theory Can Contribute to Understanding and Promoting Democracy, Science, and Development." In I. Serageldin and J. Taboroff (eds.), *Culture and Development in Africa*, vol. 1. Washington, D.C.: World Bank, 1994.

ROBERT KLITGAARD is a professor of economics at the University of Natal, Durban, South Africa.

Listening is essential to understanding, and understanding is the basis of competent evaluation. Systematic client consultation is on the way to becoming a primary ingredient of project identification and design. Systematic listening provides feedback needed for accurate and relevant evaluation.

The Listening Dimension of Evaluation

Lawrence F. Salmen

"People's knowledge," derived from living difficult lives in varying circumstances, must be the ground in which development endeavors assume meaning. As development practitioners, we need to understand how technological advances can be blended with human values so as to enhance life in a sustainable manner. To gain this understanding, there is no substitute for listening. Listening brings us closer to clients, allowing us to share experiences across cultural divides and grow together in a development that is not from one to the other but common to all.

For roughly ten years the World Bank has been engaged in an approach to development learning, based on systematic listening to clients, now known as beneficiary assessment (BA). This chapter describes this approach, presents some key findings, notes apparent advantages and disadvantages in using the approach, and suggests how development agencies can incorporate listening as part of the way they conduct, and evaluate, their business.

The Approach

Beneficiary assessment is an eclectic learning tool used to improve the quality of development operations. First used for evaluating ongoing projects, beneficiary assessment has since evolved into a tool for project design and, most recently, for policy formulation as the basic method for participatory poverty assessment. Whereas its methodology borrows more from social anthropology than any other academic discipline, its operational character allies it to consumer research and investigative journalism as well.

Four Basic Precepts. Beneficiary assessment has four basic precepts, each of which has led to particular emphases in methodology.

Increasing the Validity of Information. Truth of information is enhanced by using largely qualitative methods of research. Qualitative research is distinguished by its use of naturalistic techniques that put a premium on communication with people on their own terms, in their own language, in places where they work and live. The emphasis is on gaining the trust of the person from whom information or understanding is sought. The primary technique used is the conversational interview, either once or twice with the same person or group of persons (focus group) or repeatedly as part of a case study during participant observation, which entails living in a development site for several weeks to several months.

Being Useful to Decision Makers. This calls for involving the decision makers in the assessment at key points throughout the learning process, and particularly at the design stage, when the sampling frame and interview guide are determined. Other key points for managerial presence are during the progress review held roughly one-third of the way through the field work (enough time to derive a critical mass of findings with enough work remaining to allow for useful corrections), and at the time of the review of the first draft of the final report. Close collaboration with decision makers increases the likelihood that the findings of the assessment will in fact be used to improve the development activity.

Being Credible to the Architects of Development Programs. This is achieved by using terminology familiar to the program architects, addressing issues they consider important (such as demand), and, probably most important, quantifying the information to the degree possible, particularly via the use of representative sampling.

Directing the Learning to Make Development Interventions More Effective and Sustainable. This goes to the heart of the listening approach. In deriving an operational understanding from guided listening to clients, we enable development operations to build on the values of the people undergoing development. When a development activity is valued by the person for whom it is intended, it is presumed to be more sustainable than when it is not so valued.

What Beneficiary Assessment Is Not. Here it is important to point out two things that beneficiary assessment is not. First, it is not predominantly participatory, in the sense that its purpose is not primarily and immediately to empower. Unlike participatory rural appraisal (PRA) or other empowerment-oriented learning techniques, BA presupposes a need to provide decision makers with a credible, objective message, albeit about subjective data—something that intended beneficiaries are inherently unable to do.

Second, beneficiary assessment is not necessarily an exclusive approach to development research. Given the inherent difficulty of incorporating statistically significant sampling into in-depth qualitative approaches, it is best to combine listening approaches with more broad-reaching quantitative data-gathering methods such as household surveys. The former are more useful where the information sought is more subjective, the latter where it is more objective.

Timing. Beneficiary assessment often has been carried out as a one-off operation, either during project design or during implementation, but it is much more useful to consult systematically with clients at all stages of a project's life. True, the evaluative application of the listening may only be said to begin when there is a project to evaluate. Yet listening to intended beneficiaries before the project, at the identification stage, enables the development agent to best appreciate how to form and blend an intervention to enhance the pre-existing activity of these people.

At the other end of the project's life, the utility of the listening approach is also evident. Only through open, candid consultation with the intended beneficiaries well after (three to five years) the last disbursement has been made will a development agency find out to what degree and in what ways the project has changed people's lives.

Thus, we must learn to listen to people as soon as we imagine them to be potential clients and long after their direct involvement as project beneficiaries has ended. In this way, the listening dimension of evaluation is as geared to the culture of the people—with which a development activity must mesh to be successful—as it is to the project. As we listen to evaluate the people's own ongoing activities, we will be more able to evaluate over time how an outside intervention, project, or policy may best enhance those activities.

Bank Experience

Since 1981, the World Bank has supported at least forty-seven beneficiary assessments in twenty-seven countries covering six sectors (agriculture, urban, health, education, industry, and energy) and social funds. Beneficiary assessments constitute the single largest experience with systematic listening to clients for improving project quality in the bank's history.

Findings and Impact. Careful listening teaches one about things both obvious and unexpected. In conversations guided by topics of interest to project managers, good listeners normally gain understanding relevant to the improved working of the project. The following examples illustrate the kind of information that (1) comes out of this systematic listening approach; (2) was considered useful by project managers, in developing countries and at the World Bank; and (3) led to changes in the project. In each case, only one or two items learned are addressed; in all cases more was learned.

Urban. I begin with the urban sector because it is where this approach started, while I was living in slums in Bolivia and Ecuador where the Bank had ongoing housing and slum improvement projects. Two findings from that early period stand out. One was that the upgrading area in La Paz where I was living had a large number (close to half of the total) of renters who were not receiving the water and sewerage connections provided exclusively for homeowners under the World Bank loan agreement with the municipality. These renters had not been taken into account in the design of the project because they were invisible to the designers. Many of them lived in remote areas of the community, behind large structures or at the end of narrow alleyways. The homeowners did not talk of their own renters, perhaps out of fear that the rental income they were making might be taxed. As a renter in the community myself, I soon became aware of this other segment of the local population that was not being reached by the project. The exclusion of the renters, of course, undermined the benefits to sanitation and public health, which were the goals of the project. As a result of this finding, all future contracts between the city and the residents were with whoever resided in the houses, homeowners or renters, thus assuring greater equity and an improved urban environment.

The second finding came from my stay in Guayaquil, Ecuador. It was replicated in other World Bank–supported projects in Thailand, halfway around the world, where a later beneficiary assessment was conducted. Projects in both countries featured new housing for low-income families, which, to be more affordable, was built as unfinished core structures. The poor future residents were supposed to move into the unfinished core and complete their houses, at first with makeshift and gradually with more durable materials, as incomes permitted. Yet in Guayaquil, Chiang Mai, and Bangkok, as many as half of these structures were still uninhabited after one year of ownership. Conversational interviews revealed that people could not afford to improve their housing as they felt they should, because of their existing rental payment obligations and their concern about looking too shabby amid their better-off neighbors. This qualitative information would probably not have been elicited by questionnaires as well as it was by the combination of conversational interviews and participant observation. In both Ecuador and Thailand, at least partly as a result of these beneficiary assessments (at that time known as participant-observer evaluations), no unfinished core housing was included in subsequent low-income housing schemes.

Education. Mali has a very low rate of primary school attendance. In the late 1980s, when a beneficiary assessment was conducted there, only 15 percent of rural children went to primary school. The assessment found three reasons for this: where schools were distant, parents often had to pay for their children's lunches, which they found prohibitively expensive; parent-teacher associations generally only existed on paper; and classes were taught in French, making them too difficult for many children who only spoke their native language. As a result of these findings, a nongovernmental organization (NGO) undertook to subsidize the cost of school lunches in one region of the country, bringing about a major increase in school attendance rates; teachers were trained to build closer ties with communities via strengthened parent-teacher associations; and more classes were taught in local languages.

Health. The beneficiary assessment conducted on a health project in Lesotho revealed that community members preferred traditional healers to modern health workers, largely because the former always had curative medicines, whereas the latter often had only words about preventative health measures. As a result of this finding, the Ministry of Health made sure that all health workers had a minimal amount of supplies for curative purposes (aspirin, bandaids, and the like). Another finding, replicated in a BA in Burkina Faso and in participatory poverty assessments in Cameroon, Guatemala, and Zambia, is that poor people often avoid public health clinics because of the rude, arrogant treatment they receive from public health personnel. The Minister of Health of Lesotho noted that this finding would influence the way her country trained health workers.

Agriculture. In Senegal, for a 1994 beneficiary assessment of an agricultural extension service, local teams spent many days living in communities of farmers in representative agricultural areas of the country (cattle, groundnuts, vegetables). The training and visit (T&V) extension method being used relies on contact farmers to relay messages from the extension agent to the mass of farmers in an area. It appeared from discussions with the chief of the evaluation division of the national T&V agency, and a partial review of the data, that the contact farmers are rarely in contact with anyone except, at times, each other. Questions were raised as to the efficacy of the extension agents, most of whom were clearly held in low regard by the farmers. Here, the messages of the extensionists—like those of the health workers in Lesotho—may well have merit, but if clients do not hear them, or are not persuaded by them, their value is lost.

Social Fund. An ongoing assessment of a social fund in Zambia reveals that, in nearly one-third of the villages surveyed, one or more of the leaders of communities receiving grants (largely from another donor agency) for public works have diverted funds for their own use. This finding, bordering on that of an audit but coming out of this intensive, qualitative approach, led the World Bank to institute tighter supervision of funds in the program. A second finding concerned the interrelationship between NGOs involved with the social fund program and participation in the beneficiary communities. Certain NGOs, notably those affiliated with religious organizations, were more paternalistic than participatory, yet they managed public works well, leading to high-quality construction and sound maintenance of schools, health centers, and the like. Other NGOs, particularly parent-teacher associations, were good at fostering participation in decision making and communal activity but were found deficient when it came to the quality and maintenance of constructed or repaired work. A decision was made to pair NGOs to bring out their complementary skills towards the commonly shared end of increasing the community's ability and confidence to help itself.

Listening Assessed

Among the projects subject to beneficiary assessments, the author recalls no instance of managers criticizing the assessment adversely. On the contrary, many if not most of the managers have found the assessments useful and in some instances indispensable. The Zambian manager of the social fund referred to above said that all of the improvements in the fund in the three years since the World Bank has been supporting it were made in response to the findings of the beneficiary assessment. A regional director of the Northeast Brazil secondary cities project, after learning the findings of a beneficiary assessment done on fishing and artisan cooperatives, said that she would have this listening approach used in ten of the sixteen components of her project. The chief of research of the National Pedagogical Institute in Mali, which carried out the beneficiary assessment in education (above), said that whereas he had formerly used only quantitative questionnaire techniques, he would now use qualitative techniques in fully half of his institute's research program.

Several factors lie behind management's positive response to this listening approach to evaluation:

The information coming out of these beneficiary assessments has, with few exceptions, been found useful for improving project design or implementation.

What has been learned from operationally oriented listening has generally been seen as distinct from what is learned using traditional questionnaire (household) surveys; people recognize that a person is more apt to talk candidly in a conversational setting than to an enumerator conducting a pre-worded questionnaire.

Listening is not expensive. The forty-seven beneficiary assessments conducted to date have cost an average of $45,300, which is much less than 1 percent of total project cost.

Listening need not take long. The average time spent on these beneficiary assessments, from the first recruitment of personnel to the submission of the final report, has been 3.2 months. Given that these were almost all first experiences of their kind, subsequent assessments could probably be done in roughly two months' time.

Local knowledge is key. In all assessments except the first two (which were done by the author, with local assistance), local people conducted the beneficiary assessments—with other local people, the actual or intended beneficiaries. This compounding of local knowledge, professional and community, appears to have been widely regarded as a positive feature of this listening approach. Messages from beneficiaries are heard by the Bank and by borrowing governments because countrymen are listening to each other.

Difficulties in applying BA fall into three categories: methodological, political, and cultural. *Methodological* difficulties are the easiest to deal with. People trained to use questionnaires—as are most social analysts in developing countries—tend to go in two directions when presented with this kind of qualitative, listening approach. Either they stick with what they know, use a questionnaire, and call it an interview guide or, conversely, they go all the way to pure description, thinking—erroneously but understandably—that qualitative research means "no numbers." Good training and good selection of personnel will take care of these problems. The best practitioners of beneficiary assessments have been lawyers, architects, economists, social workers, journalists, and psychologists, as well as anthropologists and sociologists. The key ingredients for a good and useful listener appear to be empathy, communication skills, and sound, practical experience with development programs in the field.

The *political* problems are more difficult, but nevertheless avoidable. Staff turnover can erode the continuity or applicability of this kind of innovative and potentially threatening learning. More sensitive than turnover is the issue of trust. The high degree of trust that is needed for intensive-listening approaches is not always present. The only two beneficiary assessments to be suppressed had been done under dictatorial and insecure regimes, without involving top government officials in the decision making process at the outset.

The *cultural* factors mainly concern the internal culture of the World Bank itself. Much has already been said over the past few years about the need for the World Bank to profoundly adapt itself to the kind of listening, learning stance exemplified by beneficiary assessments. Bank president Preston's call for increasing ownership among borrowers and his related urging to staff to be client-oriented are moving in the direction of the listening approach described in this chapter. With the support being given in the World Bank's Africa Region to systematic client consultation, which grew out of the BA approach, and with growing interest in participatory poverty assessments in most regions of the Bank, a change is at work.

Looking Ahead

Given the widely acknowledged value of feedback from clients for quality work, it is highly recommended that ongoing evaluation using the listening, BA approach recommended here become the norm rather than the exception in development projects. Experience with those BAs that have played this evaluative role, even if at only one point in time but especially where done iteratively, has shown the cost-effectiveness of incorporating ongoing evaluations as an aid to project implementation.

Second, development assistance agencies need to encourage the strengthening of client countries' capacity for conducting evaluations that capitalize on listening techniques. Providing this encouragement is not easy. A government's wish to institutionalize listening might be construed by key segments of the population (including the political opposition) as an admission that public institutions fail to listen adequately to the people they are supposed to serve. Following from this, staff of assistance agencies may be uncomfortable foisting what might be perceived as intrusive, politically sensitive policy guidance on wary country personnel. Nevertheless, as seen above, listening can be presented as being in the best interests of all concerned—a kind of reality check or consumer research approach, which, if done well, should improve the quality and sustainability of development programs, and avoid the embarrassment and adverse backlash of failed efforts.

If assistance agencies and client country governments can increase countries' capacity to carry out this listening approach, institutional and individual reservoirs of talent will be created and may be drawn on to help client country managers, assistance agencies, and, ultimately, the communities themselves. Pilot efforts to institutionalize this listening within countries would help to avoid starting from scratch each time a new BA or PRA commences in a given country. Depending on the particular country context, this institution building could take place with indigenous NGOs, research institutes and universities, or within government bodies.

Evaluation may best be viewed as catalytic learning. We evaluate programs and policies by listening to the key actors so that these people can better transform their worlds to meet their own aspirations. Evaluation, then, has the effect of bringing about change not as an end but as a means for people, both managers and intended beneficiaries, to first understand what change is wanted and possible and then, over time, assess whether that change is indeed enriching the lives of those for whom it is intended.

LAWRENCE F. SALMEN is senior social scientist in the Environment Department of the World Bank.

A survey of citizens of Bangalore asked what they thought of the public utilities and related agencies that delivered the city's essential services. The survey findings shed light on the state of the public services in Bangalore and show how "voice" mechanisms can be used to demand better service and greater accountability from public service suppliers.

Evaluating Public Services: A Case Study on Bangalore, India

Samuel Paul

The efficiency and effectiveness of public services in a country are important determinants of the productivity, progress, and quality of life of its people. Industry and commerce cannot thrive and expand when infrastructure services such as power, water, transport, municipal services, and communications are inadequate and inefficient. Entrepreneurs tend to incur high costs and to avoid long-term commitments when faced with such problems. Governments control and supervise important infrastructure sectors not only because of the large-scale nature of their operations and the immense funds required to run them but also because the public and often monopolistic nature of the services necessitates careful regulation and monitoring. That more than 50 percent of the public investment in India's Eighth Five Year Plan is devoted to infrastructure sectors is not surprising. This chapter refers to the services of these sectors as "public services" and the service providers and utilities involved as "public agencies."

Public services in the urban areas of India are widely believed to be unsatisfactory and for the most part deteriorating. They are managed and regulated by authorities and corporations established by the government. As public agencies, they operate under certain political and administrative constraints that often do not apply to private enterprises of similar size. In many cases, the rapid expansion of urban areas has added to their burden without a corresponding expansion of resources. But the poor performance of these agencies

---

An earlier version of this paper appeared in *Economic and Political Weekly* of India.

cannot necessarily be attributed solely to these factors. According to well-informed observers, the monopolistic nature of the services, inadequate oversight and corrective actions by government, and the lack of organization and collective action by citizens for better service have combined to stifle the agencies' responsiveness to the public and their motivation to improve services even within the limits of available resources.

Background

Many studies have been carried out on public sector and public agencies in India, but most are concerned with the overall economics, finance, and management of the enterprises, and the majority take a governmental or managerial perspective. By contrast, this study presents a view of the public services from the citizens' perspective. Because users are at the receiving end, their assessments of the quality, efficiency, and adequacy of the public services and the problems they face in their transactions with public agencies can provide significant input for the improvement of service delivery and management of the agencies involved. Enterprises and agencies operating in a competitive setting tend to pay special attention to feedback from their customers. Products and services often are redesigned, and pricing, promotion, and other organizational practices reformed in light of such feedback. But, as noted above, the monopolistic nature and organizational incentives of most public agencies limit their concern for soliciting or using such feedback. A user perspective or a "view from below" is thus a sadly neglected dimension in urban public services as well as in many other areas in India.

This study of citizens' assessments of public services in India focuses on Bangalore, a city of 4.5 million people, with an impressive network of scientific research institutions and high-technology commercial ventures. Despite Bangalore's growing importance as a center of commerce and technology, its public services and service providers basically suffer from the same shortcomings as those in India's other large urban centers.

The basic questions driving the case study are threefold: How satisfactory are the public services that matter most to the citizens of Bangalore? What specific aspects and features of their working are satisfactory or unsatisfactory? What does it cost the users to get the services or to solve the problems associated with getting services? The answers to these questions shed light on the prevailing patterns of service-related problems, users' concerns about the weaknesses of the service agencies, their attitude toward corruption in the agencies, and their views on possible remedies.

When citizens assess services and agencies based on their interaction with agency staff, they make it possible to rank the agencies by service performance. This exercise produces an interesting byproduct—an organizational "report card" that can be used to stimulate introspection by agency managers and the public at large. Even though the information underlying user ratings is subjective and incomplete, there is no gainsaying the fact that public perceptions matter, especially when clear patterns emerge from analysis of experiences of large numbers of people. When users identify a problem with a specific service, the feedback allows the agencies and the government to correct the problem (if the problem is found to exist) or to educate the public (if there has been a misunderstanding).

Scope and Methodology

This case study consists of six components: a random sample survey of 807 households in Bangalore, in-depth interviews with a select group of professionals working on industrial and commercial projects in the city, focus group discussions with slum dwellers, mini case studies of selected respondents, documentation of the information provided to the public by service providers, and interviews with a sample of lower level staff of the agencies. The methods used ranged from statistical surveys to qualitative interviews, focus groups, and participant observation. Thus the study used both quantitative and qualitative research methods to arrive at its findings.

The household survey was undertaken to obtain systematic feedback on the public's experience with the various service providers and on their assessments of the adequacy and quality of the services. Bangalore's residential areas were stratified by age of locality. Six areas were then randomly selected from among the old and established, intermediate, and new. The areas were Chamrajpet, Frazer Town, Koramangala, Malleswaram, Richmond Town, and Sanjaynagar. From each area sample households were selected using random numbers, with the condition that the household have had interactions with one or more public-service agencies during the preceding six months. From among the estimated 800,000 households in Bangalore, more than 2,000 were contacted, yielding a sample of 807 households that met this criterion. Trained investigators administered the detailed structured questionnaires. The survey was completed in the last quarter of 1992.

Entrepreneurs and commercial investors are required to get approvals and permits for their industrial and commercial projects in Bangalore and its surrounding areas. To assess business peoples' experience with public service agencies, six leading professionals were interviewed in depth. Although only a few people were interviewed, the scope of their work covered a substantial share of the industrial and commercial investment projects in the area. They were questioned not only about the nature and quality of the services, but also on the impact of recent economic reforms on the regulations and controls exercised by the agencies.

Bangalore has a slum population of more than 470,000 (about 10 percent of the population). Because a questionnaire survey was considered inappropriate for this population, investigators held focus group discussions in the slums adjacent to the selected residential areas. From the six large slum areas thus identified, eight focus groups were organized, each of which met with trained investigators for more than an hour. The subject of the survey was made known to the people in the slums, and informal groups of four to five persons interested in talking about the subject were formed, with the investigator facilitating a semistructured discussion. In all, about forty slum dwellers shared their experiences and concerns about public services through focus groups. This is by no means a statistically valid sample. Nevertheless, the insights and patterns of problems highlighted by the groups were valuable in generating important hypotheses for further exploration.

Of the 807 households covered by the sample survey, eighteen were selected for in-depth interview based on their willingness to elaborate on their experiences with public service agencies. These mini case studies provided insights and examples that would have been difficult to capture through the structured questionnaire survey. The in-depth interviews also permitted the respondents to offer solutions to the problems they encountered. Of the mini case studies, twelve pertained to experiences with building a house, a complex endeavor requiring interaction with multiple public agencies.

To observe the kind of information and guidance made available to the public, the investigators visited the service providers with whom the respondents interacted the most. Investigators introduced themselves as customers. They asked for information on how to obtain specific services and on the procedures involved. The public information displayed in the offices and the responses of the staff were noted. The primary purpose of the investigation was to assess how readily and to what extent information was provided (or denied) to the public to facilitate (or limit) service delivery. These observations of the trained investigators provided a cross check on citizens' feedback on the quality of service.

A small number (twelve) of the lower- and middle-level staff from selected public agencies were interviewed for their perspective on service delivery and the problems they encountered in dealing with the public. Because the staff interacted daily with the public, investigators believed that the "view from the other side" could shed useful light on the topic and lead to a more balanced analysis and interpretation of the public's assessment of the service providers. The sample included field staff, such as line workers, meter readers, and valve openers from the selected localities, and clerical staff from some of the agency offices. Trained investigators interviewed agency staff, who were identified on an ad hoc basis in the field and in offices.

Of the six components of the study, the sample survey was the largest and most time consuming. The sample size implies extremely tight error ranges at the overall level. The standard error of the sample estimated using the lowest sample split is no more than 3.2 percent. This means it can be said with 90 percent confidence that any sample finding is within 5 percent of its actual occurrence in the universe. This is the worst case scenario; in most cases, the actual margin of error is likely to be much lower.

Major Findings

Relative Importance of the Public Agencies to Citizens. The study did not focus on a predetermined set of agencies or services. Instead, respondents were asked to identify the agencies they had dealt with in the preceding six months to solve a problem or to obtain a service. Forty-nine percent of respondents had dealt with the Karnataka Electricity Board, and 34 percent had had transactions with the Water and Sewerage Board. Other agencies identified were the Bangalore Municipal Corporation (19 percent), public sector banks (16 percent), public hospitals (13 percent), the Regional Transport Office (12 percent), Bangalore Telephone (10 percent), the Bangalore Development Authority (6 percent), and such agencies as post and city transport (19 percent). Totals add up to much more than 100 because some households had interacted with more than one agency. The post and city transport agencies were excluded from further analysis because the number of observations by agency was not large enough for statistical purposes. Based on the sample responses, it was reasonable to conclude that these agencies were of less importance for citizens in terms of the problems they encountered with service providers. In all cases, respondents were asked to comment only from personal experience over the preceding six months.

What were the main reasons citizens contacted public service agencies? They contacted Karnataka Electricity Board mainly to sort out excess billing, to have power restored, and to request repairs and sanctions. They contacted the Water and Sewerage Board for similar reasons and to complain about irregular supply. People contacted the Bangalore Municipal Corporation primarily for tax matters, land title changes, garbage clearance, and sanctions. Transactions with banks were mostly for routine services and in a few cases for loans. Visits to hospitals were for out-patient and in-patient care and for treatment of accidental injuries. The Regional Transport Office was contacted for vehicle licenses and tax payments. Interactions with Bangalore Telephone concerned mostly excess billing, repairs, and new connections. Citizens dealt with Bangalore Development Authority on tax matters, site allotment, and sanctions.

The vast majority of the interactions were through personal visits. Eighty-six to 98 percent of contacts with seven out of eight categories of the service providers were done this way. The proportion was smaller for Bangalore Telephone, which had 47 percent of contacts through visits and 31 percent by phone. A single visit was seldom enough to obtain a satisfactory response or service. In the case of the Bangalore Development Authority, 95 percent of the respondents claimed to have visited its offices two or more times to address a problem. The percentage was lower (35 percent) in banks, where people went mostly to make routine transactions.

In 50 to 65 percent of the cases, respondents had to meet two or more officials to resolve a problem. In a third to two-thirds of the cases people had to also meet the supervisor to resolve their problem.

What do these patterns signify about the management of those agencies? It is clear that for the average person interacting with these agencies, almost no work gets done by phone or mail. Even those who write in must follow up with visits. For working people everywhere, personal visits are costly, inconvenient, and time consuming, particularly in a busy city, and to have to visit offices several times and meet with several officials is even more costly and aggravating and a poor use of everyone's time. Yet respondents gave many examples of how officials would unhesitatingly ask them to "come back tomorrow" because the file could not be found or because the official involved was unavailable. The fact that such unproductive practices continue unchecked, especially when 75 percent of cases are relatively simple to resolve, is symptomatic of weak supervision, callousness, corruption, widespread public tolerance, or a mixture of all four.

Agency Report Card. Respondents were asked to rate the level of their satisfaction with the public agencies they had interacted with. They were asked not only for an overall assessment based on their recent experience but also about specific aspects of the service, for example, behavior of staff and quality of information given to them. To make their responses comparable across agencies, they were asked to choose a point on a scale of 1 to 7 that approximated their views, one representing extreme dissatisfaction and seven representing highest satisfaction (see Table 11.1). Though people's judgments partly depend on their expectations about a service, this aspect of the assessment was not explored in the study, so no attempt could be made to adjust individual assessments against corresponding expectations.

The end product of such a scaling technique is a set of scores by respondents that can be used to rank and compare the public's rating of agency services. Because people are at the receiving end of services, they seldom have an opportunity to signal the agencies on what they think of them. The aggregation of their scores for the first time fills this gap. In fact, this score card amounts to respondents' "collective voice," provided it is heard and used. The public's assessment may not always be correct. What is important is that it signifies their perceptions of the agencies in a way that individual complaints or legal cases can never do. Such assessments go beyond anecdotes about public agencies to reveal patterns from numerous experiences. The results reported below need to be viewed in this light.

Even the better rated agencies such as banks and hospitals generated a satisfaction score of only 20 and 25 percent respectively. The proportion of those dissatisfied far exceeded that of the satisfied except in one case (hospitals). Further analysis of staff behavior revealed "inability to respond quickly" and "lack of enthusiasm in helping" as two major weaknesses across all agencies.

When asked whether they would pay higher official fees for public services to ensure service, more than 54 percent of the respondents expressed a willingness to pay. Higher-income persons were clearly more willing to pay,

Table 11.1. Overall Public Satisfaction, by Agency

	Average Rating	Percent Satisfied[a]	Percent Dissatisfied[b]
Bangalore Development Authority	2.5	1	65
Bangalore Municipal Corporation	2.9	5	49
Water and Sewerage Board	3.0	4	46
Karnataka Electricity Board	3.5	6	31
Regional Transport Office	3.5	14	36
Bangalore Telephone	3.6	9	28
Banks	4.0	20	26
Hospitals	4.3	25	19

1–Very dissatisfied; 2–Dissatisfied; 3–Somewhat dissatisfied; 4–Neither satisfied nor dissatisfied; 5–Somewhat satisfied; 6–Satisfied; 7–Very satisfied.

[a]Percent Satisfied = Total of 6 and 7

[b]Percent Dissatisfied = Total of 1 and 2

but even among the lower-income groups, nearly 50 percent of the respondents seemed willing to pay the higher fees for services. This finding challenges some of the conventional assumptions about people's willingness to pay for public services. Important policy implications follow from this finding.

Information Barriers. Visits to agency offices by trained investigators to assess the quality of information available to the public revealed a mixed picture. Some of the offices displayed helpful information, but their staff were not enthusiastic about giving further guidance. A classic case is that of property taxation by the Municipal Corporation. The criteria and methods for determining this tax are not explicit and are not known to most taxpayers. The public has accepted it as a negotiable tax, with the public exchequer probably losing much money. In one case, it took an investigator four visits to three different offices to get a copy of a printed and priced pamphlet. Some public agencies even treat their annual reports as internal documents and do not make them readily accessible to the public.

This part of the study revealed a significant finding: that most public agencies responsible for serving Bangalore citizens are not "citizen friendly." They do not seem to view citizens as clients to be served. Offices and internal systems are not designed for ease of service or efficient problem solving. Agencies' indifference to information as an aid to the public may be a consequence of their monopoly condition or, as some argue, a deliberate means to extract speed money. Lack of public information in effect raises a barrier to citizens' ability to access public services.

A major implication of the evidence from diverse sources is that the supply response (new investment, higher production, improved efficiency) that policy makers hope will follow in the wake of the recent reforms in India may not materialize or may emerge more slowly than expected because of the problems identified above. Good macroeconomic management is unlikely to improve the economy's performance without necessary microlevel actions to augment the supply of goods and services. If new investments do not come about or factories remain underutilized because of inefficient infrastructure and unresponsive public utilities, the focus of attention will have to shift to a search for new strategies to reform the latter or to find new substitutes for them. Pressure from the public should be seen as a force in support of this move. A strong case thus exists for mobilizing the feedback and participation of the public in the process of reforming public service agencies at the local level.

Conclusions and Implications

A number of conclusions follow from the findings of the public evaluation. First, levels of public satisfaction with the performance of Bangalore's public agencies are noticeably low across the board. Even the better performers such as banks and hospitals have not elicited ratings beyond 25 percent. Considerable scope exists for improving the performance of all the public agencies involved.

Second, an evaluation of public services using citizen feedback provides valuable insights that a conventional economic evaluation, for example, cannot offer. Under monopoly conditions where citizens do not "exist," an economic evaluation may well yield a high rate of return for a public service, but it would be inappropriate to conclude from that evaluation that the service is efficient or effective. Users may pay for the service because they have no option, not because they are fully satisfied.

Third, an evaluation based on citizen (user) feedback can provide useful inputs for improving the accountability and overall performance of public agencies. Public assessment of the different dimensions of a service (for example, quality, reliability, and staff behavior) may yield comparative data that can be used to further diagnose agency problems and to seek answers or remedies. This explains why forward-looking governments are beginning to ask their public agencies and departments to conduct periodic surveys of customer sat-, isfaction.

The findings of the study have some important implications for the government and the public at large. Supply shortages (for example, water and power) cannot fully explain the prevalence of poor responsiveness to the public or the corruption found in the public agencies. Many so-called shortages are created or manipulated by withholding information or through the use of arbitrary procedures. Although the Regional Transport Office and Bangalore Municipal Corporation do not generally deal with services that are in short supply, the services covered in this study represent the most measurable part of the government's output. Public utilities are "production" organizations with definable outputs or products. Yet no one defines or monitors their services, not because no one is capable, but because it is not high on anyone's agenda. A start can be made by introducing greater transparency in the working of these agencies and by providing users with helpful information so they can demand better services and challenge abuses. Agency regulations and procedures, particularly those that may have been in force for a long time, need systematic review and simplification with the participation of the public and outside experts. A process of debureaucratization needs to be started without delay, taking into account the feedback from the public. The great merit of such reform is that it does not require much money, and it will help reduce opportunities and incentives for corruption. Reforming the system, however, calls for strong political commitment.

Imaginative approaches to the pricing of public services deserve special attention in light of the finding that citizens are willing to pay higher official fees in return for efficient services. The time has come to think about such options as "dual tracks" for services. This option has already been tried to some extent by a few public agencies (telephones, for example). The faster track would entail higher official fees and would be designed to meet the needs of those who want quicker service delivery. The slower track may take longer, but the norms for completion should be transparent and adhered to. The extra incomes agencies accrue with this option could be used partially to reward employees for good performance. A major challenge is to demonstrate distinct improvement in services while raising fees—a complex task—but details can be worked out once consensus is reached at the policy level.

Citizens have traditionally left to the government the task of devising and enforcing public accountability for its performance, but government's role and services have expanded considerably in recent years, making it difficult to achieve accountability through conventional mechanisms such as audit and legislative reviews. Collusion, abuses, and lack of responsiveness to citizens' needs in numerous public agencies cannot be easily detected and rectified, even with the best of supervision. Public choice theory has provided considerable evidence on this subject (Paul, 1992).

These problems are not unique to the public sector. Poor service and neglect of customers can be found in the private sector as well. More likely, both public and private producers of goods and services are used to an environment that encourages indifference to the customer. In the private sector, competition can take care of this problem over time. But changing public-sector behavior calls for more imaginative approaches. Under these circumstances, the public has to play an active and ongoing role in monitoring public services that are of direct concern to them. Civic groups can play a useful role in educating the public about services and more generally about civic behavior, thus making it easier for public agencies to serve the people.

The results of this evaluation illustrate the kind of public feedback that can be generated and used to demand better and more responsive public services in a city. Mobilizing the voice of the people requires collective action, however. Citizens should realize that they must go beyond individual complaints and influence seeking to collective action (for example, through local resident associations or other forums), which will give them the power and continuity both to monitor and change the quality of public services. But the incentives for collective action are not always strong in this area. For example, while 62 percent of the citizens interviewed said they would like to join a civic association, only 38 percent felt that they would actively participate in it. Lack of civic organizational efforts and reluctance of citizens and officials to collaborate for problem solving are major weaknesses in India's urban areas.

Well-organized local groups can be influential in accelerating the kinds of reform discussed above. The media can play a constructive role in support of these efforts. Public services are too important to be left to public servants alone.

The monopolistic nature of the public services discussed in this study is at the heart of the problem of the inefficient and nonresponsive behavior found in public agencies. An obvious remedy would be to seek alternatives to current service delivery modes and to find creative ways to instill a sense of competition in the sectors involved. Some agencies, such as the Bangalore Municipal Corporation, have already begun to explore these avenues and to adopt modest steps to reduce monopoly power in services. But when all is said and done, the role of the government and of its agencies in public services is likely to remain significant. Since competitive alternatives cannot easily be created and sustained in this setting, competition should be stimulated in other ways, fully recognizing that the interest groups that benefit from the prevailing regime will not easily give up.

One promising approach is to conduct periodic well-publicized intercity evaluations of the performance of public service agencies. Such evaluation would be a means to inform and goad governments to take action and to strengthen the hands of local groups to demand better service and accountability from their public agencies. Individual complaints and legal action against public agencies can have a salutary effect and need to be continued with rigor, but they are no substitute for systemic reforms. For example, that 25 percent of Bangalore citizens have excess billing problems with three major agencies illustrates a serious systemic problem. Although some improvements can be made in the short run, reforms in the selection and training of staff, incentives for staff, supervision and monitoring, and measuring devices and accountability at all levels may be needed to resolve the problem. When systemic reforms are put in place, the magnitude of individual complaints should decline.

Reference

Paul, S. "Accountability in Public Services: Exit, Voice and Control." *World Development*, July 1992.

SAMUEL PAUL is chairman of the Public Affairs Center, Bangalore, India.

Based on the prior chapters, this postscript pulls together a framework for improving the interface between evaluation and development.

Postscript: Development Questions and Evaluation Answers

Ray C. Rist

The chapters in this volume have an interesting duality about them. They provide a strong sense of consensus around certain issues but raise challenging questions on others. Their contributions in pinpointing areas of agreement and disagreement help to identify gaps in the relation between development and evaluation and to throw light on the challenges facing evaluators working on development issues.

This volume is not a reconsideration of the new development agenda itself. Broad agreement on that agenda has been hammered out through policy research, development evaluation, international debate, and action in the field. What is offered here is an assessment of where evaluation fits (and where it does not) within the context of the new agenda. Although the analytical, conceptual, and political framework of development has changed dramatically, it is not clear at this point that evaluation has responded appropriately to this change. In this sense, the volume is an assessment of the potential for a rapprochement.

What areas of consensus have emerged? First, the authors take for granted that a shift is taking place in the long-established focus on the "project" as the unit of analysis for assessing development impacts and consequences. The new development agenda calls for broader understandings of sectors, countries, development strategies, and policies.

Second, the emphasis within the new development agenda on listening to people, and on working to ensure they have a voice in the development process, raises the profile of participatory evaluation. The call for participatory evaluation comes at a time when the distrust of "official" data in many developing countries is so high that what governmental data systems and databases do exist have little or no legitimacy. The moral and methodological bankruptcy of data systems in the former communist countries is but a case in point. The corruption of the system did not stop at the boundaries of evaluation. The result is that participatory evaluation takes on an additional justification in that the data generated from such an approach are believed to be more trustworthy, more accurate, and less manipulated by government officials. Whether participatory evaluation can withstand the corrupting influences of governmental intervention and control remains to be seen.

Third, the demand for new methodologies and a different mix of skills goes beyond economics and draws from all the social sciences. The study of cultural context, of institutional change, and of the means of empowerment are but three examples of the kinds of topics that need to be considered by development evaluators. With the decline of development economics as the preeminent paradigm for the assessment of activities has come a more diverse and broadly based evaluation approach. Despite the consensus that new methodologies and a different mix of skills are necessary, there is no illusion that these will come readily or soon. The extreme limitations on any form of evaluation data collection and the building of data systems will not be reversed overnight. The compounding effects of linguistic heterogeneity within countries and the lack of a social science infrastructure or tradition in country after country are but two among many constraints that make even rudimentary data collection so difficult. Simply stated, the evolution of the evaluation community into one where design and methodological approaches are more broadly based will take sustained effort for a decade or longer.

Fourth, the special problems of the environment call for new and innovative evaluation approaches. The scope of environmental problems, their multinational consequences, the difficulties in obtaining comparable measurements, and the persistent evidence of unanticipated consequences (what Hirschman calls "the centrality of side effects") all necessitate a complex and multimethod approach to evaluation.

Fifth, many of the present practices for evaluating development projects, programs, and policies are described repeatedly as inappropriate, irrelevant, and sometimes just plain wrong. The diagnosis as to why is blunt: the development evaluation community has not stayed abreast of the changing needs inherent in the new development agenda. As a subtext on this same theme, the findings imply that the persistent efforts to export first world evaluation strategies to the developing world may need to be reconsidered. (Indeed, many of the present strategies employed in developed countries are also being vigorously challenged. The status quo holds nowhere.)

As to the areas of disagreement in this volume, for some of the issues and questions raised here, even the debate has yet to be well framed. With the advent of a more demanding, fragmented, and participatory approach to development, evaluation has become much more difficult to design. It encompasses more intricate methodological demands and sets very different standards for establishing impacts. In this context, definitive answers are elusive. To reiterate Robert Picciotto's point from the introduction to this volume:

> It may well be that no single discipline can be expected to dominate in an endeavor that deals with the multiple challenges, hopes, and exertions of the majority of humankind. In the absence of a single intellectual rallying point, trespassing across disciplinary boundaries is common and evaluators are increasingly eclectic and venturesome in their use of social science instruments.

This said, the chapters in this volume have an undercurrent of sober optimism that knowledge and practice are linked, and that evaluation is the necessary bridge between them. The new development agenda emphasizes learning and continuous feedback at all phases of the development cycle. In this context, evaluation is viewed as the centripetal force holding the two in a necessary tension with one another, helping to keep the development system together by providing consistent incentives and enhancing accountability. But for this potential to be tapped, current evaluation practices need reevaluation.

Issues Challenging Evaluation in the New Development Context

Five themes in particular emerge from the chapters in this volume as ripe for reconsideration. Though these do not pretend to exhaust the key points of the chapters, or of the multiple perspectives and issues disclosed at the December 1994 conference where the chapters were discussed in draft form, the intent here is to isolate some important and persistent dilemmas at the intersection of evaluation and development—and to suggest a framework for further discussion.

Evaluation Designs for Development Efforts. The manner in which evaluation questions are framed has a significant impact on the subsequent evaluation design. In particular, the persistent emphasis in the development community on asking what have been the economic impacts of development efforts—via cost/benefit analysis—pushed the evaluation function into a highly positivistic and quantitative mode. In the transition now underway within development evaluation, the movement away from microeconomic analysis has gone in multiple directions. As noted above, there are calls for changing the scope of analysis away from projects and programs to broader sectoral and thematic concerns, more participatory designs and involvement in evaluation, and more qualitative approaches. But although at one level there may be a tendency to let a thousand flowers bloom, the development evaluation community appears to be converging towards more interest in and focus on consistent standards for judging development impact.

Here, the term "impact" takes on the meaning of finding out what has happened to real people in real places, how development efforts have affected these people, what efforts yield sustainable benefits, and whether and how local ownership of the project or program has taken hold. Impacts are no longer defined as a priori benefit projections or the hypothetical outcomes of a model; they are the documented outcomes of one or a cluster of interventions. Further, not all impacts are assumed to be beneficial; negative impacts are increasingly a focus of investigation.

A note of caution is needed. An impact evaluation is the most difficult type of evaluation to design and conduct. Among the well-documented threats to validity are the difficulties in establishing reliability, the presence of "false positives" and "false negatives," the difficulties of establishing adequate measurement of projects that are "weak thrust, weak effect," the absence of adequate comparison or control groups, the absence of adequate baseline data, and the difficulties in eliminating competing explanations for any documented outcomes. It will be difficult to meet the expectations of donors and borrowers that evaluations can and should be designed to determine cause and effect relations for many if not most development initiatives.

Hence, the authors of this volume are not unanimous on the feasibility (or even the desirability) of using impact evaluations to establish cause and effect relations between development initiatives and changes in people's lives. Impact studies are expected to provide more verifiable and concrete information to enhance learning and thus improve future initiatives. Yet the jury is still out as to just how successful this new emphasis will be in providing useful insights for decision makers.

Based on experience, it would appear that the development community should be asking for a mix in evaluation designs and in the types of questions that evaluations are expected to answer. Although an emphasis on impacts is legitimate and challenging, a case also can be made for asking more modest questions of evaluators, and for being willing to accept more modest answers. More attention is needed to issues of implementation, to documenting different strategies of local participation and empowerment, to ensuring that the voice of the people is heard in assessing a development initiative, and to studying the cultural context of development initiatives. Such questions stand in contrast to impact or cause and effect questions, and they lend themselves to evaluation designs that are more easily executed as viable evaluation studies, at acceptable costs.

The prior chapters also make clear that evaluators should not try to answer impact or cause and effect questions without a sound research base, and a judgment, based on thorough understanding of the issues, as to whether such answers are even possible.

Evaluation Methods. Beyond issues of evaluation design, authors and conference participants questioned whether current evaluation approaches employ methods appropriate to the design questions and are appropriate to the changing context and direction of the new development agenda. Some believe that present methods are ill-suited to many design questions. Others believe that present approaches are increasingly missing the point of what is happening in development.

As to the first concern, something of a divide is emerging within the evaluation community between those who hold to a largely economic model for evaluating projects and those who argue that an equally viable set of issues can be evaluated with approaches entirely separate from economics. Within the economic framework, emphases on rates of economic return are preeminent. It is against such benchmarks that projects are assessed and subsequently judged successful or not. Literature is abundant on economic criteria and approaches to the assessment of development projects, programs, and policies, but as with any approach that has been so dominant for so long, a growing set of detractors is able to point out its limitations and failures. Development economics is not defunct, but it lacks the intellectual or institutional credibility it held just a few years ago.

Evaluation specialists who argue for a fundamentally different approach emphasize the cultural context in which development does or does not take place. This preoccupation with context takes multiple forms—an interest in historical and cultural factors, a focus on the social and political processes of development, a concern with project and program implementation so that one "knows" what has actually been implemented before one begins thinking about measuring outcomes, and arguments for more participation of local people at the project level in both defining and assessing project goals—to name but a few examples.

An unfortunate tendency has been to frame the debate in an "either-or" mode, not recognizing the complementarity between the two approaches. The distinction is akin to the difference between a positivistic and a phenomenological view of knowledge, or between quantitative and qualitative ways of conducting inquiry. The chapters in this volume do not seek either to narrow or to widen the differences between these two co-existing approaches. Neither does the volume suggest a specific strategy for obtaining a suitable mix of approaches or tapping their potential synergies. By moving beyond the assumption of an inevitable schism, however, it encourages the evolution of a new, more encompassing frame of reference for crafting development evaluations.

What such a frame should include will be the subject of considerable discussion, but clearly evaluation and economics will have to find new common ground, perhaps in the area of the new institutional economics. In addition, one can speculate, more emphasis will be placed on the use of multimethod approaches to assessing development, where qualitative and quantitative methods will find themselves partners in answering the evaluation questions implicit in the new development agenda.

Evaluators and Evaluating Organizations. Embedded in this volume are a number of points related to the professionalization and identification of those we call evaluators. The calls for participatory evaluation recognize that local people, traditionally thought of as the targets of development efforts, need instead to be co-participants in designing, implementing, and indeed, evaluating these same projects and programs. The emphasis here is on empowering local people to more actively participate in efforts to shape their future.

What is less discussed and proposed is how such people are to be selected, trained, and sustained in their efforts over time so that the capability is not soon lost. This demands a long-term capacity building strategy, a coordinated approach to development evaluation standards among different organizations, and a support system, both within individual countries and internationally. Building a social-science-based evaluation capability will take time, money, training, and willingness on the part of people in developing countries to devote themselves to such a career path.

From a different slant and with a slightly different rhetoric, there is also an emphasis on building capacity at the local level for conducting evaluations. The presumption is that with the changing nature of the role of evaluation in studying development, there is a crucial need for local expertise to enrich and inform evaluations, particularly those that are longitudinal and focused on matters of implementation.

The matter of building and sustaining local capacity goes beyond that of generating expertise: organizational capacity is needed to address systematic data collection over time, to build databases, establish baseline data systems in areas where new development programs will be initiated, and strengthen the ability to conduct panel surveys. Further, as the calls continue for more contextual data collection, more listening to people being affected by the development initiatives, and—not to be underestimated or ignored—more systematic project and program monitoring, there will have to be an organizational capability to respond.

The development community is asking simultaneously for new and different types of evaluations to be conducted in developing countries and for more local participation and involvement. To build this kind of infrastructure and expertise and sustain it over time will be no mean feat. Indeed, many industrialized countries still lack this capacity. Though the return on investment in evaluation capacity may be higher in developing countries than in the industrialized countries, expectations of quick success need to be tempered by a realistic perspective on developed country experience.

Who Needs Evaluation? Interestingly, this volume says little about present or future demand for evaluations. It is often declared that better quality should lead to greater use, but this is said more as an aspiration than as a statement of either the present condition or of empirical truth. Further, the sources of demand—present or future—receive only sporadic attention.

The demand issue is tricky for several reasons. First is the matter of the source of demand. Donor organizations, borrowing government agencies, and different local implementation organizations can all reasonably expect evaluation information to help them in their respective responsibilities. Should accountability be the major preoccupation and therefore should structural independence be the overwhelming priority in the first instance? Or, if the lesson-learning dimension is given preference, should the first ring of users be among the policy makers in developing countries? Or again, should priority be given to those most responsible for actually managing and implementing projects and programs? They are, after all, the group at the front lines and on whose shoulders falls the responsibility to achieve the promised development objectives.

The volume provides little guidance on how to decide such questions, but the authors do suggest that with such different potential end-users, the evaluation function will face quite different demands. If the development system heretofore was relatively stable and closed, it is now open, transparent, and full of new actors. The implications for the evaluation function are manifold.

The Use (and Abuse) of Evaluation. Finally, we come to the link between demand and use. Demands for evaluation after evaluation, data analysis after data analysis, may be motivated by a genuine desire to learn from experience, or merely by the need to meet a bureaucratic requirement, with no intention of using the gathered information. If the demand is genuine, evaluation information will potentially be used to help improve projects and programs. This kind of instrumental use can contribute over time to sustaining the commitment of people conducting evaluations and can help to improve the quality of the evaluation information. This is the hope with which most people come into the evaluation field. However, if information is merely being collected as a bureaucratic ritual, there is little reason to expect any quality in the data, any motivation on the part of those generating the information to ensure accuracy, or any substantial trust in the enterprise.

At least two other types of use should be considered. One is conceptual use, for which evaluation material helps to reframe an issue, clarify the understanding of a program or problem, and help those in the policy arena to think about a situation in new ways. This is perhaps the way in which evaluations are most often used, but it is very difficult to track and measure. The other type of use is political, for which the evaluation material helps reinforce or challenge support for a policy or program. Evaluators often are flattered when their material gets this kind of visibility and publicity, but the use (and abuse) of their work is out of their hands, and their work may be used for reasons they do not endorse or may not even suspect.

The chapters in this volume are framed toward instrumental use. The assumption is that evaluation information and analysis can inform program and project improvements as well as enhance learning at the policy level. The aspirations for evaluation are high. The belief in its usefulness and its utilization is comforting, even if somewhat overstated.

The final point about use is the schism between evaluators and policy makers noted by Eleanor Chelimsky. These two groups frame issues differently. They respond to different sets of pressures and incentives, and they may be organizationally isolated from one another. The result is often that they do not share a common understanding of the issues being evaluated, and consequently they talk past one another. To recognize these "two worlds" is to face up to the challenge that the gap between them must be bridged in order to secure value for evaluation.

A Final Note

The chapters in this volume come to terms with the transformation necessary for evaluation to become a full partner in the new development agenda. Evaluation brings a particular set of skills and perspectives to bear on ascertaining the relevance, consequences, and the efficiency of development interventions in the lives of individuals and societies.

Undoubtedly evaluation has considerable potential to participate actively in this process, but development evaluation capacities are still not up to the task. Fundamental shifts are needed in the entire life cycle of the evaluation endeavor. Issues of design, data collection and analysis, decision making and information dissemination processes, and the presumption of use, all need reconsideration. This special issue is only a first step on a journey whose challenges are profound and systemic for the global evaluation profession.

RAY C. RIST *is director of the Center for Policy Studies, Graduate School of Education and Human Development, the George Washington University.*

INDEX

Accountability: and development economics, 16; for public services, 163
Ackerman, P. L., 141
Adrian, J., 83, 90
Africa, sociocultural settings in, 143
Agency for Technical Cooperation (GTZ), Germany, 139
Agricultural/rural development (ARD) programs: and beneficiary assessment, 151; causal logic of, 85; characteristics/settings of, 83-85; and conceptualization of results, 85; evolving nature of, 83-84; and limited organizational capabilities, 84-85; and macroeconomic policy, 115; and performance indicators, 81-82; and performance measurement system, 82; and PMS model, 82-83, 85-90. *See also* Participatory rural appraisal (PRA)
Aharoni, Y., 57
Ake, C., 143
American Academy of Arts and Sciences, 14
Amsberg, J. von, 74
Anand, R., 42
Anderson, M., 110, 112
Angel, S., 124
Ascher, W., 72, 75
Askew, J. M., 102
Assessment: of cultural factors, 141-142; gender-needs,113; impact,21; institutional quality, 63-64. *See also* Beneficiary assessment (BA); Evaluation
Assignment model, 40-42
Au, K. H., 138
Austin, J., 110, 112

Bamberger, M., 29
Bangalore (India) public services evaluation (case study): background of, 156-157; basic questions of, 156; and citizen feedback, 160-162; findings of, 159-162; implications of, 162-165; and intercity evaluations, 164-165; and monopoly power, 164; and pricing strategies, 163; and public accountability, 163; and public agency assessment, 160-161; and public agency-citizen relationship, 159-

160; scope/methodology of, 157-158; and supply shortages, 163
Beck, T., 108, 113
Beneficiary assessment (BA): and agricultural projects, 151; cultural difficulties with, 153; defined, 33, 147; and education projects, 150; and health projects, 150-151; listening approach to, 151-154; methodological difficulties with, 152; nonparticipatory/nonexclusiveness of, 148; political difficulties with, 153; and poverty alleviation programs, 32-33; precepts of, 147-148; and social fund programs, 151; and timing, 149; and training-and-visit-extension method, 151; and urban sector projects, 149-150; and World Bank projects, 149-151
Beneria, L., 112
Berk, R. A., 98
Berlage, L., 70
Binnendijk, A., 90, 105, 106
Bishop, J. H., 103
Boggs, S., 138
Bolivia: beneficiary assessment in, 149-150; poverty alleviation programs in, 28-29
Borouch, R. F., 35
Borries, L., 70
Boserup, E., 112
Bourgoin, H., 143
Bradburn, N., 102
Britan, G. M., 83
Buijsrogge, P., 143
Buvinic, M., 107

Canadian Council for International Cooperation/Match International, 112
Capacity building: and development economics, 17; and environmental projects, 75; for evaluators, 172
Carpenter, R. A., 72
Carter, S., 143
Carvalho, S., 113
Casley, D. J., 81, 87, 89, 90, 106
Cassen, R., 105
Centre International des Civilisations Bantu, 143

Ordering Information

NEW DIRECTIONS FOR EVALUATION is a series of paperback books that presents the latest techniques and procedures for conducting useful evaluation studies of all types of programs. Books in the series are published quarterly in Spring, Summer, Fall, and Winter and are available for purchase by subscription as well as by single copy.

SUBSCRIPTIONS for 1995 cost $56.00 for individuals (a savings of 22 percent over single-copy prices) and $78.00 for institutions, agencies, and libraries. Please do not send institutional checks for personal subscriptions. Standing orders are accepted. (For subscriptions outside of North America, add $7.00 for shipping via surface mail or $25.00 for air mail. Orders *must be prepaid* in U.S. dollars by check drawn on a U.S. bank or charged to VISA, MasterCard, or American Express.)

SINGLE COPIES cost $17.95 plus shipping (see below) when payment accompanies order. California, New Jersey, New York, and Washington, D.C., residents please include appropriate sales tax. Canadian residents add GST and any local taxes. Billed orders will be charged shipping and handling. No billed shipments to post office boxes. (Orders from outside North America *must be prepaid* in U.S. dollars by check drawn on a U.S. bank or charged to VISA, MasterCard, or American Express.)

SHIPPING (SINGLE COPIES ONLY): one issue, add $3.50; two issues, add $4.50; three to four issues, add $5.50; five issues, add $6.50; six to eight issues, add $7.50; nine or more issues, add $8.50.

DISCOUNTS FOR QUANTITY ORDERS are available. Please write to the address below for information.

ALL ORDERS must include either the name of an individual or an official purchase order number. Please submit your order as follows:
  Subscriptions: specify series and year subscription is to begin
  Single copies: include individual title code (such as PE59)

MAIL ALL ORDERS TO:
  Jossey-Bass Publishers
  350 Sansome Street
  San Francisco, California 94104-1342

FOR SUBSCRIPTION SALES OUTSIDE OF THE UNITED STATES, CONTACT:
  any international subscription agency or Jossey-Bass directly.